FOCUS on Literacy

Teacher's Resource Book 2

Barry and Anita Scholes

Collins

Author: Karina Law

Design: Grasshopper Design Company; Amanda Easter

Editor: Janet Swarbrick

Cover image: Kelvin Murray, Tony Stone Images

Illustrations: Maggie Brand, Rob Mooney

Published by Collins Educational
An imprint of HarperCollins*Publishers* Ltd
77-85 Fulham Palace Road
Hammersmith
London W6 8JB

Browse the complete Collins catalogue at
www.collinseducation.com

www.harpercollins.co.uk
Visit the book lover's website

First published 1999
20 19 18 17 16 15 14 13 12

ISBN-13 978-0-00-302518-7
ISBN-10 0-00-302518-7

British Library Cataloguing in Publication Data
A catalogue record for this book is available from the British Library.

Printed in Great Britain by Martins the Printers, Berwick-upon-Tweed

Contents

Focus on Literacy and the National Literacy Strategy

You will find in ***Focus on Literacy*** a strong support in the teaching of reading and writing within the context of a literacy hour. All the literacy objectives of the National Literacy Strategy for each term may be covered by using the Big Book anthologies together with the Pupil Book, the Homework Book, the Copymasters and the Teacher's Resource Book. Here, in one grand design, are sufficient teaching materials for five full literacy hours per week throughout the entire school year.

The aims of *Focus on Literacy*

The aims of ***Focus on Literacy*** are identical to those of the National Literacy Strategy: to develop each child's ability to read and write. It promotes their development by honing the literary skills necessary to meet the Range, Key Skills, and Standard English and Language Study of the National Curriculum Programmes of Study.

These skills are wide-ranging and specific, and worthy of review:

- to read and write with confidence, fluency and understanding
- to use a full range of reading cues (phonic, graphic, syntactic, contextual) to self-monitor their reading and correct their own mistakes
- to understand the sound and spelling system and use this to read and spell accurately
- to acquire fluent and legible handwriting
- to have an interest in words and word meanings, and to increase vocabulary
- to know, understand and be able to write in a range of genres in fiction and poetry, and understand and be familiar with some of the ways that narratives are structured through basic literary ideas of setting, character and plot
- to understand and be able to use a range of non-fiction texts
- to plan, draft, revise and edit their own writing
- to have a suitable technical vocabulary through which they can understand and discuss their reading and writing
- to be interested in books, read with enjoyment and evaluate and justify preferences
- to develop their powers of imagination, inventiveness and critical awareness through reading and writing.

The NLS framework and *Focus on Literacy*

The NLS teaching objectives for reading and writing are set out in termly units to ensure progression. Each term's work focuses on specific reading genres and related writing activities. ***Focus on Literacy*** offers carefully selected examples of these reading genres and stimulating activities relating to them.

The overall structure is the same for each term and is divided into three strands: text, sentence and word levels. Text level refers to comprehension and composition, sentence level to grammar and punctuation, and word level to phonics, spelling and vocabulary. The activities in ***Focus on Literacy*** offer many opportunities for the development of handwriting, while leaving you free to follow your school's own writing policy.

The literacy hour and *Focus on Literacy*

The NLS framework requires a literacy hour as part of school work each day. The literacy hour is designed to establish a common pattern for all classes and is carefully structured to ensure a balance between whole class and group teaching, as the diagram below shows.

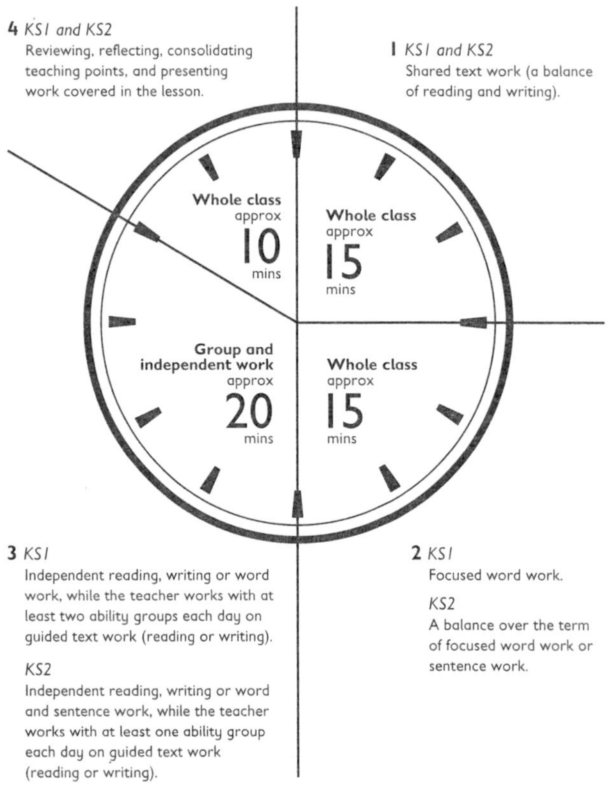

This structure enables you to spend up to 100 per cent of your time in direct teaching. Children work in a direct teaching relationship for approximately 60 per cent of the time and independently for the remaining 40 per cent.

The high-quality texts of *Focus on Literacy* and the related activities directly meet the NLS objectives, and so relieve you of the burden of deciding *what* to teach. The teacher's notes support you in planning *how* to use the materials in your teaching.

Shared whole class time

Shared whole class time takes place during the first half of the literacy hour. It is divided into 15 minutes of shared text work (a balance of reading and writing) and 15 minutes of focused word and sentence work. This is the time when you can effectively model the reading/writing process with the children.

In shared reading you can help to extend reading skills in line with the NLS objectives, teaching and reinforcing grammar, punctuation and vocabulary.

The reading texts also provide ideas and structures for shared writing. Working with the whole class, you create the opportunity to teach grammar and spelling skills, to demonstrate features of layout and presentation, and to focus on editing and refining work. The shared writing will also be the starting point for independent writing.

Independent activities

The shared whole class time of the literacy hour is followed by 20 minutes of independent activities. During this time you will probably work with a guided reading or writing group, while the children will be working independently, but within a group organised by ability to cater for differentiation.

Each section is short so that children will be able to complete the activities you select in the time available. The Homework Book is available for those who finish early and wish to keep busy, as well as for work outside the classroom. Other activities which the children may do during this time are independent reading and preparing presentations for the class.

It is suggested that you aim to work with each guided reading and writing group for two sessions per week, organised so that you see each child in the class at least once.

Plenary

The final 10 minutes of the literacy hour is a plenary session for reviewing, reflecting upon and consolidating teaching points, and presenting work covered in the lesson. This is an essential element of the hour. It is important to plan this activity so that every child has the opportunity to feed back once as part of their group during the course of a week. A different objective will be featured each day so that each objective is reinforced in turn. This will allow you to monitor each group's progress and highlight the teaching/learning points as necessary.

Using *Focus on Literacy*

The Big Book anthologies

There are three Big Book anthologies, each covering a term's work. These consist of carefully chosen texts for shared work on word, sentence and text levels. The extracts also provide the context for the independent activities. Each unit provides texts for a week's shared reading.

Each extract is accompanied by a *To think and talk about* section to prompt and stimulate the children's responses.

Further teaching points and suggestions are given in the Teacher's Resource Book.

The Pupil Book

The Pupil Book is made up of 30 units. Each unit begins with the main text and is followed by the independent activities for the week.

To help you with differentiation, the independent activities are identified for level of difficulty, section B generally offering a higher level of challenge than A. Each section is scaled to a workable size.

The five-day spread

Day 1: the independent activity is text-based. Section A has questions for literal recall, while most in section B are inferential. The questions in the *To think and talk about* section are intended as shared reading questions in order for you to help the children to explore the text at greater depth and prepare them for tackling the independent questions.

Days 2 and 3: independent activities focus on word, sentence or text work.

Days 4 and 5: shared writing is followed by independent writing.

"Stickers" provide the children with the facts they need to complete the work and make the most of the activities.

The Homework Book

The Homework Book contains activities which consolidate and extend the work in the Pupil Book. This book is equally useful in the classroom outside the literacy hour and out of the classroom for work at home.

The Teacher's Resource Book

The Teacher's Resource Book comprises notes, copymasters, including assessment masters, and record sheets. It also outlines a basic approach to each unit in the Big Books and Pupil Book and includes an award certificate.

The teacher's notes and you

The teacher's notes help you use the ***Focus on Literacy*** material to the best advantage. The notes are arranged in five sections, each covering one literacy hour. These are further subdivided according to the literacy format: shared text/shared writing work, focused word/sentence work, independent work, and plenary.

A termly planning chart introduces each group of ten units. This chart lists the range of texts for that term, the word, sentence and text work which is explicitly covered, and the continuous work which will be part of your teaching throughout the term, such as practising reading and spelling strategies.

The teacher's notes for each text are organised to facilitate the literacy hour.

A *Key Learning Objectives* box lists the key literacy objectives covered in that week's work, and a *Resources* box identifies the range of texts covered, details of the extracts, and the page references of all the components used in the unit.

Details are given of any special preparation you need to do for the unit, for example providing dictionaries.

The *Shared reading* section lists teaching points and suggestions on how to explore the meaning of the text, in line with the literacy framework objectives. In fiction and poetry this entails exploring genres, settings, characters, plots, themes, figurative language, authorship and the way different texts are organised. In non-fiction text this involves genres, structures and presentation, identifying main points, skimming and scanning, exploring steps in a process and comparing different sources.

The texts often provide both structure and content for writing activities, and the context for many of the activities at sentence and word level on the Copymasters.

The *Shared writing* section offers guidance on how texts are composed. The main text studied in earlier shared reading sessions will provide the ideas and structure for this writing. Each shared writing activity is the starting point for subsequent independent writing.

The *Focused word/sentence work* section offers appropriate teaching points and suggestions for investigating text in detail to explore how its message is influenced by style: language, grammar, choice of vocabulary and presentation. Pupil Book 2 supports independent consolidation of the work.

The *Independent work* section introduces the independent reading, writing or word and sentence activities which may be found in Pupil Book 2, Homework Book 2 or on Copymasters.

The *Plenary* section has suggestions for reviewing and reflecting upon the work covered, consolidating teaching points and presenting work.

A *Consolidation and extension* section has ideas and suggestions for follow-up activities.

The *Homework* section describes the related activity in Homework Book 2.

Copymasters

The Copymasters offer a range of support material among which are book reviews, planning sheets, character profiles, writing frames, consolidation and extension work.

Assessment

To facilitate assessment there is an assessment master for each term.

Record keeping

Record sheets are provided at the back of the Teacher's Resource Book. They feature a summary of the term's objectives, each with a space for your comments.

Award certificates

A photocopiable award certificate is provided to reward significant individual achievements in literacy.

Basic approach to each unit

The basic approach to each unit in ***Focus on Literacy*** is as follows:

Day 1

Shared **reading** of a text in the Big Book.

Focused word/sentence work based on the shared text.

Independent text work on the shared text, which is reproduced in Pupil Book 2.

Plenary session for which there are suggestions in the teacher's notes.

Day 2

Further shared **reading** of a text.

Further focused word/sentence work based on the text.

Independent word, sentence or text work in Pupil Book 2.

Plenary suggestions in the teacher's notes.

Day 3

Further shared **reading** of a text.

Focused word/sentence work based on the text.

Independent word/sentence work in Pupil Book 2.

Plenary suggestions in the teacher's notes.

Day 4

Shared **writing**, using the shared text as a model or stimulus.

Focused word/sentence work, appropriate to the shared writing task.

Independent writing, using guidance in Pupil Book 2.

Plenary suggestions in the teacher's notes.

Day 5

Shared **reading** of a text in the Big Book.

Focused word/sentence work based on the text.

Continuation of the independent writing from Day 4.

Plenary suggestions in the teacher's notes.

This approach is flexible, occasionally varied to make the most of the week's activities.

Work outside the literacy hour

The Copymasters and Homework Book provide activities for outside the literacy hour and outside the classroom.

The extracts in ***Focus on Literacy*** are only part of the genre coverage. You will need time outside of the literacy hour to read aloud to your class, giving children the opportunity to hear complete stories, novels and poems. You will also need to show them complete non-fiction texts, so that features such as covers, blurbs, information about authors, contents, indexes and chapter headings can be discussed and appreciated. Children will need further time for their own independent reading for interest and pleasure.

You can help to reinforce genre features when children choose books for independent reading, or during guided reading sessions when you are working with a group.

Big Book contents

BIG BOOK 2A TERM 1

BIG BOOK 2B TERM 2

BIG BOOK 2C TERM 3

Pupil Book contents

TERM 1

TERM 2

TERM 3

Homework Book contents

TERM 1

TERM 2

TERM 3

Copymaster checklist

TERM 1

	Copymaster	
General	1	Look, Say, Cover, Write, Check
Unit 1	2	Something I Have Learned
Unit 2	3	New Shoes
Unit 3	4	How to Annoy Your Big Sister
Unit 4	5	Sorry Miss . . .
Unit 5	6	My Special Day
Unit 9	7	Instructions
Unit 10	8	Make Your Own Angel
	9	Angel Template

TERM 2

Unit 11	10	The Frog Prince
General	11	Passport
Unit 12	12	Glossary
Unit 13	13	Dog, Cat and Monkey
Unit 14	14	My Favourite Food
Unit 15	15	My Dictionary of Food
Unit 16	16	Manji and the Raja
Unit 17	17	*ch* as in "School"
Unit 18	18	Snake Charm
Unit 19	19	Dragon Mountain
Unit 20	20	Badger

TERM 3

Unit 21	21	Julian and Huey's Surprise
General	22	Character Profile
Unit 23	23	Question Wheel
Unit 27	24	Riddles
Unit 29	25	Kitchen Machines
Unit 30	26	Little Red Riding Hood and the Wolf
General	27	Story Report
Term 1	30	What Did I Learn This Term?
Term 2	30	What Did I Learn This Term?
Term 3	30	What Did I Learn This Term?

Focus on Literacy Achievement Award

Record sheets: Year 2, Term 1
Year 2, Term 2
Year 2, Term 3

Teacher's Notes

Year 2 • Terms 1–3

TERM 1

HALF-TERMLY PLANNER

Year 2 • Term 1 • Weeks 1–5

SCHOOL ____________________ **CLASS** ________ **TEACHER** ______________

		Phonetics, spelling and vocabulary	Grammar and punctuation	Comprehension and composition	Texts
Continuous work **Weeks 1–5**		WL 5, 6, 9, 11, 12	SL 1, 4	TL 1, 2, 9	**Range** **Fiction and poetry:** stories and a variety of poems with familiar settings **Non-fiction:** instructions
Blocked work **Week**	**Unit**				**Titles**
1	1	WL 1, 8 10	SL 5	TL 6, 7, 8, 10	From *The Magical Bicycle*, Berlie Doherty, Collins; *My New Bike*, Georgie Adams
2	2	WL 10	SL 2, 5	TL 4, 6, 7, 8, 10, 11, 12	*Street Sounds*, Jacqueline Brown; From *Tales of A Fourth Grade Nothing*, Judy Blume
3	3	WL 1, 2, 3, 8	SL 5	TL 4, 5, 6, 15, 18,	From *The Pain and the Great One*, Judy Blume
4	4	WL 2, 3	SL 5	TL 6, 11	From *Sorry Miss*, Jo Furtado
5	5	WL 3, 4, 10	SL 2, 5	TL 4, 6	From *Granny's Quilt*, Penny Ives

TERM 1

HALF-TERMLY PLANNER

Year 2 • Term 1 • Weeks 6–10

SCHOOL ____________________ **CLASS** ________ **TEACHER** ______________

		Phonetics, spelling and vocabulary	Grammar and punctuation	Comprehension and composition	Texts
Continuous work **Weeks 6–10**		WL 6, 9, 11, 12	SL 1, 4	TL 1, 2, 9	**Range** **Fiction and poetry**: stories and a variety of poems with familiar settings **Non-fiction**: instructions
Blocked work **Week**	**Unit**				**Titles**
6	**6**	WL 1, 2, 3, 4, 7	SL 5	TL 5, 6, 10	From *Tall Inside*, Jean Richardson
7	**7**	WL 3, 10		TL 5, 6	From *Snowy*, Berlie Doherty, Collins
8	**8**	WL 3, 4, 7	SL 2, 3	TL 3, 4, 5, 6, 10	From *A Worm's Eye View*, Jan Mark
9	**9**		SL 6	TL 13, 14, 15, 16, 17, 18	From *Kitchen Fun*, Ray Gibson; *Making a Christmas Tree*
10	**10**	WL 7	SL 2, 3, 5	TL 3, 4, 5, 13, 14, 16, 18	From *Josie Smith at Christmas*, Magdalen Nabb, Collins

Unit 1 A New Bicycle

Key Learning Objectives

TL6	to discuss familiar story themes and link to own experiences
TL7	to learn, re-read and recite favourite poems, taking account of punctuation; to comment on aspects such as word combinations, sound patterns (such as rhymes, rhythms, alliterative patterns) and forms of presentation
TL8	to collect and categorise poems to build class anthologies
TL10	to use story structure to write about own experience in same/similar form
WL1	to secure identification, spelling and reading of long vowel digraphs in simple words from Y1 term 3
WL8	to secure understanding and use of the terms *vowel* and *consonant;*
WL10	to learn new words from reading linked to particular topics, to build individual collections of personal interest or significant words
SL5	to revise knowledge about other uses of capitalisation, e.g. for names, headings, titles, emphasis, and begin to use in own writing

Range:	Fiction and poetry: stories and a variety of poems with familiar settings
Texts:	From *The Magical Bicycle*, Berlie Doherty, Collins *My New Bike*, Georgie Adams
Resources:	Big Book 2A pp. 4–8 Pupil Book 2 pp. 4–5 Homework Book 2 p. 2 Copymaster 2

Preparation

- Day 5: you will need Post-it® notes, or something similar, to cover specific words in the text.

DAY 1

Big Book 2A pp. 4–5; Pupil Book 2 pp. 4–5

Shared reading

- Introduce the extract from *The Magical Bicycle* by Berlie Doherty which begins on page 4 of Big Book 2A. Read through the first page with the class.
- Ask the children what the little boy's "best surprise" is. What did the boy hurt when he fell off the bike?
- Look at the illustration on page 5 of Big Book 2A together. Ask why the little boy is wearing a helmet. Discuss the safety issues which need to be taken into account when riding bicycles.
- Read page 5 of Big Book 2A with the class. Ask who is helping the little boy. What advice does he give? What does the little boy dream about at night?
- Ask the children to predict whether or not the boy will ever learn how to ride his bike.
- Discuss with the children where they would like to ride a bicycle if they had one.

Focused word/sentence work

- Look at the way the extract is set out as a poem rather than a story. Is it a poem? Remind the children that poetry does not have to rhyme! Do the children think the author has chosen her words carefully? Which lines do they like best?
- Look at the title of the poem on page 4. Which word describes the bicycle?
- Turn to page 5 again. What is "the entry"?
- Look at the words spoken by Dad. Point to the speech marks that contain Dad's speech and ask the children to read his words aloud.
- Look at the words spoken by the little boy. Read them aloud together. Can the children explain why the word "WILL" is printed in capital letters? Read the line again, placing greater emphasis on the word "WILL".

Independent work

- The comprehension questions on page 5 in Pupil Book 2 are based on the extract the children have shared with you during this session.

Plenary

- Read through page 5 of Big Book 2A again with the class. This time, choose two children, one to read the words spoken by Dad, the other to read the words spoken by the little boy.
- Encourage the children to discuss with the class the things that they find difficult, e.g. swimming, tying shoe-laces.

DAY 2

Big Book 2A pp. 4–6; Pupil Book 2 p. 5

Shared reading

- Re-read pages 4–5 of Big Book 2A with the children to remind them of the story extract.
- Turn the page quickly and read the first line on page 6. Did the children expect the little boy to fall off again? Continue reading to the end of this page with the class.
- Discuss what the children think will happen next.

Focused word/sentence work

- Turn back to the beginning of the extract and ask the children to read the first few lines to you. Write the following sentence on the board: *My best surprise was my bike but I couldn't ride it.* Underline the *i* and the *e* in *surprise, bike* and *ride.* Ask the class to say with you the long *i* vowel sound.
- Focus on the word *bike.* Can the children make new words by changing the onset? Offer clues if the class are unable to think of many words, e.g. *hike, like, spike.* Repeat this exercise with the word "ride" e.g. *bride, side, slide, wide.*

Independent work

- The exercises on page 5 of Pupil Book 2 focus on the long *i* vowel sound (as in *bike*).

Plenary

- Say aloud a number of words containing *i-e* and one word containing the short *i* vowel sound, e.g. *bike, nice,* *pin, twice*. Ask the children to listen carefully and tell you the odd word out.
- The boy in the story thinks that there might be a magic word which would enable him to ride his bike. Ask the children to offer suggestions as to what that special word might be.
- Talk about the idea of being able to do something by magic. If it was possible, what would the children like to be able to do?

DAY 3

Big Book 2A pp. 4–7; Pupil Book 2 p. 5

Shared reading

- Read the entire story extract, from beginning to end, with the class.
- Talk about how it felt once the little boy was able to ride his bike by himself. Can the children think of times when they have felt this way?
- Look at the final lines on page 7. Do they seem familiar to the children? Re-read the lines on page 5 that refer to the little boy's dream.

Focused word/sentence work

- Revise yesterday's work on words containing *i-e*. Write a rime on the blackboard, e.g. *-ice, -ime, -ine* and generate a list of rhyming words by encouraging the class to change the onsets.
- Using page 7 of Big Book 2A, ask the children to count the number of times on the page that they can see the pronoun *I*. Listen to the long vowel sound when you say the word aloud. Remind the children that they should always use a capital letter for *I*. Can they tell you of the other occasions when a capital letter should be used?

Independent work

- Use this time to complete the exercises on page 5 of Pupil Book 2, focusing on the long *i* vowel sound (as in *bike*).

Plenary

- Re-read the following lines from page 5 of the extract and then write them on the board:

  "But every night, deep in my dreams
  I rode my bike. . ."

  Ask the class to help you think of other ways to complete this imaginatively.

DAY 4

Copymaster 2

Shared writing

- Encourage the class to think about something which they have found/are finding difficult to do. It might be swimming, playing the recorder, tying shoe laces or something else that they remember well.
- Ask the children to talk about their feelings. Who helped them? How much practice was needed? How did they feel when they finally got the hang of whatever it was they were struggling to do?
- It might be useful to begin by writing down a few phrases or words offered by the children during your class discussion.

Focused word/sentence work

- Discuss ways of beginning a piece of writing about this theme, bearing in mind that the children will be choosing different topics. Write useful sentence openers on the board for the children to use as a writing frame for their own ideas, e.g. *Something which I found difficult to do was. . .; I needed to. . .; I was helped by. . .; In the end I. . .; I felt . . .*
- Once you have established a structure, ask a volunteer to "fill in the gaps" orally with you.

Independent work

- Provide each child with a copy of the writing frame (Copymaster 2) to assist them in writing about an experience of their own. More able children may like to deviate from the given frame. More time is allowed on Day 5 for the completion of this task.

Plenary

- Choose volunteers to read aloud their work. Discuss how useful the children have found the sentence starters. Do they need to change the wording of any? Would they like to add any new sentence openers?

DAY 5

Big Book 2A p. 8; Copymaster 2 from Day 4

Shared reading

- Before you begin to introduce the poem by Georgie Adams on page 8, cover the words *stop* and *today*. Read through the poem with the class, encouraging them to supply the hidden words as you reach them.
- Talk about the mentioned features of the bike: its gears, brakes, bell and handlebars. Discuss the function of each.
- Can the children think of any other features of a bicycle which are not mentioned here, e.g. saddle, lights, chain, pedals? Can they point to any of these in the illustrations?

Focused word/sentence work

- Uncover the hidden words to see if the children guessed them correctly. Perhaps they thought of alternatives which worked equally well.
- Show how the word *handlebars* is made up of two smaller words by covering first *handle* and then *bars* and asking the class to read aloud the words that remain. Repeat this exercise for the words *birthday* and *everyone*.
- Write the words *shop* and *stop* on the board. Underline the rime *-op*. Ask the children to think of new words by changing the onset, giving clues if necessary, e.g. *chop, crop, drop, flop, hop, mop, top*.
- Generate a list of words that rhyme with *way/today*.

Independent work

- This time could be used by the children for either completing or redrafting their writing based on personal experiences of learning a new skill.

Plenary

- Discuss with the class the best features of each child's work.
- Help the class learn *My New Bike* and recite it from memory, taking into account the rhyme and rhythm of the poem during its performance.

Consolidation and extension

- Read *The Magical Bicycle* by Berlie Doherty in its entirety.
- Ask the children to look for other poems about bicycles to make a class collection.
- Look at labelled diagrams of bicycles in non-fiction books to identify the gears, brakes, handlebars, and other main features.

Homework

- Page 2 in Homework Book 2 focuses on identifying main features of a bicycle and riding a bicycle safely.

Unit 2 Shoe Shuffle

Key Learning Objectives

TL4	to understand time and sequential relationships in stories
TL6	to discuss familiar story themes and link to own experiences
TL7	to learn, re-read and recite favourite poems, taking account of punctuation; to comment on aspects such as word combinations, sound patterns (such as rhymes, rhythms, alliterative patterns) and forms of presentation
TL8	to collect and categorise poems to build class anthologies
TL10	to use story structure to write about own experience in same/similar form
TL11	to use language of time to structure a sequence of events, e.g. *when I had finished . . ., suddenly. . ., after that. . .*
TL12	to use simple poetry structures and to substitute own ideas
WL10	to learn new words from reading linked to particular topics
SL2	to find examples, in fiction and non-fiction, of words and phrases that link sentences, e.g. *after, meanwhile, during, before, then, next, after a while*
SL5	to revise knowledge about other uses of capitalisation, e.g. for names, headings, titles, emphasis, and begin to use in own writing

Range:	Fiction and poetry: stories and a variety of poems with familiar settings
Texts:	*Street Sounds*, Jacqueline Brown From *Tales of A Fourth Grade Nothing*, Judy Blume
Resources:	Big Book 2A pp. 9–13 Pupil Book 2 pp. 6–7 Copymaster 3 Homework Book 2 p. 3

DAY 1

Big Book 2A pp. 9–10; Pupil Book 2 pp. 6–7

Shared reading

- Begin by asking the children to talk about the different kinds of footwear that they like to wear. Introduce the poem, *Street Sounds*, by Jacqueline Brown which begins on page 9 of Big Book 2A.
- Read through the first two verses of the poem on page 9 with the class. Ask the children questions relating to the text: What noise do the wellies make? Who is wearing flip-flops? What sort of noise do the flip-flops make?
- How many children in the class own a pair of wellies? How many have worn flip-flops before? When would it be appropriate to wear these types of footwear?
- Turn to page 10 and read the remainder of the poem with the children. Who is wearing high heels? Who is wearing slippers?

Focused word/sentence work

- Read through the first two verses on page 9 again with the class. Which word in the poem rhymes with *feet*?
- Compare verses one and two. What is similar? What is different? Draw the children's attention to the repetitive pattern.
- Look closely at the poet's choice of words. Point out the alliteration in the first verse: "Blobble blabble" and "wobbly wellies". Can the children find words close together in the second verse which begin with the same sounds (*flip-flops, slit-slap, slittery slappery*)? Talk about the way these words sound when put together.

Independent work

- The questions on page 7 of Pupil Book 2 relate to the poem, *Street Sounds*, by Jacqueline Brown. Children who complete this work might like to think of their own words to describe the sounds the different types of footwear shown on page 7 of Pupil Book 2 would make.

Plenary

- Try re-reading the verses, replacing the onomatopoeic words with other words that the children think describe the sounds of the footwear effectively. Provide further challenge by changing the types of footwear (e.g. trainers, rollerskates, flippers).

DAY 2

Big Book 2A pp. 9–10; Pupil Book 2 p. 7

Shared reading

- Re-read the poem, *Street Sounds*, by Jacqueline Brown with the class.
- Can the children tell you which of the four characters in the poem is moving most quickly along the street? Who is probably moving the most slowly?
- Choose volunteers to demonstrate how each of the characters is moving, focusing on the words *walking, running, parade* and *shuffles*. Read each verse again as the corresponding mime is being demonstrated.

Focused word/sentence work

- Focus on page 10 of Big Book 2A. Read the first word, *listen*. Can the children find another word on the page which has a similar meaning?
- Ask the children to find words close together which share the same sound: *high heels, clock clop, snorey slippery*.
- Encourage the class to invent other words to describe the sound of Mum parading in her high heels and Grandma shuffling in her slippers.

Independent work

- The exercises on page 7 of Pupil Book 2 focus on alliteration.

Plenary

- Try performing the poem with actions to accompany the first, second and third lines of each verse.

DAY 3

Big Book 2A pp. 11–12; Pupil Book 2 pp. 6–7

Shared reading

- Introduce the story extract from *Tales of A Fourth Grade Nothing*, by Judy Blume, which begins on page 11 of Big Book 2A.
- Read through page 11 with the class. Why does Mr Berman measure *both* of Peter's feet?
- Read through the rest of the extract on page 12. What is Peter's mother embarrassed about? How does Peter try to hide the hole in his sock? How many pairs of shoes did he try on? What was wrong with the first pair?
- Encourage the children to talk about their experiences of trying on new shoes. Do they enjoy shopping for shoes? Do they help choose the shoes they would like to wear? Perhaps they have had their shoes bought for them from somewhere other than a shoe shop, e.g. a catalogue or a market stall. Ask them to describe their favourite pair of shoes.

Focused word/sentence work

- Ask the children to find the different uses of capitalisation on page 11 (title, names, beginning of sentences and the personal pronoun, *I*).
- Look at the first paragraph on this page. Can anyone tell you how many sentences there are in this paragraph? Ask a volunteer to point out where each sentence begins and ends. Can anyone see a comma? Remind children that a comma does not mark the end of a sentence, but a pause within it. Read the sentence together, pausing when you reach the comma.
- Look at other punctuation marks on the page. Can anyone find a question mark? Can anyone find an exclamation mark? Talk about the function of each.
- Divide the class into two. Instruct one half of the class to read the words spoken by Peter on pages 11 and 12 and the other half to read Peter's mother's words. Point out the speech marks that contain the spoken words.

Independent work

- This time is allocated for the completion of the exercises on page 7 of Pupil Book 2.

Plenary

- Invite children to read the sentences they have written describing the shoes on page 7 of Pupil Book 2. Discuss what is best about each description.

DAY 4

Pupil Book 2 p. 7

Shared writing

- Read through the instructions given on page 7 in Pupil Book 2. Discuss the questions orally with the whole class. Write down key words and phrases.
- Think about ways of beginning a sentence to answer each question. You might like to begin in this way: *I needed new shoes because . . . , so my . . . took me to . . . to buy me a new pair.*
- Use a volunteer to answer each question posed on page 7 while you act as a scribe.

Focused word/sentence work

- Think of ways to make the writing more interesting. Choose a volunteer who has had his/her feet measured to describe this process. How many pairs of shoes were tried on before a suitable pair was chosen?
- Choose another volunteer to tell you how his/her experience differed from the first child's. Show how the writing format can be adapted to accommodate the new set of answers.

Independent work

- Ask the children to each write an account about buying new shoes based on their own experiences. Children who do not recall ever having been to a shoe shop could write an imaginary account based upon the experiences they have heard discussed.

Plenary

- Choose one or two children to read their accounts so far. Discuss the best features of the writing. Help them to develop any incomplete sentences.
- Explore a role-play situation. Ask the children to work in pairs, one child in each pair playing a child trying to persuade a parent to buy a pair of high-fashion shoes while the other child plays the parent, who wants to opt for a more sensible, less fashionable pair. Encourage the children to explain exactly why they like one pair more than the other. As you are watching the children, choose one or two pairs to re-enact their role-play situations to the rest of the class. Discuss any issues that arise from the drama.

DAY 5

Big Book 2A pp. 11–13; Pupil Book 2 p. 7; Copymaster 3

Shared reading

- Re-read the extract from *Tales of a Fourth Grade Nothing*. Look at and discuss the sequence of events in this extract: Peter has his feet measured by Mr Berman; then Mr Berman goes to look for shoes in Peter's size; Peter tries on two different pairs; he chooses the pair that fits best; finally Mr Berman wraps the shoes for Peter to take home. Write these events in shortened form on the board.

Focused word/sentence work

- Look closely at the phrases/sentences you have written on the board. Discuss whether or not they could have been presented in a different order. Why not? Try swapping a few sentences around to see what effect that has on the structure of the story.
- Focus on the words *then* and *finally*. Discuss why the word *then* could not be used to begin the first sentence. Why could *finally* not be used to open any sentence other than the last?

Independent work

- The children should use this time to complete the writing they began on Day 4.

Plenary

- Hide the sentences that you wrote on the board during the shared reading session and organise the children for paired work. Hand out a copy of Copymaster 3 to each pair. Ask them to cut out the jumbled sentences and arrange them into the correct order.

Consolidation and extension

- Read further extracts to the class from Judy Blume's *Tales of A Fourth Grade Nothing.*
- Ask the children to look out for other examples of alliterative poems.

Homework

- Page 3 in Homework Book 2 focuses on alliteration and explaining a preference.

Unit 3

The Pain and the Great One

Key Learning Objectives

TL4	to understand time and sequential relationships in stories
TL5	to identify and discuss reasons for events in stories, linked to plot
TL6	to discuss familiar story themes and link to own experiences
TL15	to write simple instructions
TL18	to use appropriate register in writing instructions, i.e. direct, impersonal, building on texts read
WL1	to secure identification, spelling and reading of long vowel digraphs in simple words
WL2	to revise and extend the reading and spelling of words containing different spellings of the long vowel phonemes from Year 1
WL3	the common spelling patterns for the vowel phoneme *oo* (short as in *good*)
WL8	to secure understanding and use of the terms *vowel* and *consonant*
SL5	to revise knowledge about other uses of capitalisation, e.g. for names, headings, titles, emphasis, and begin to use in own writing

Range:	Fiction and poetry: stories and a variety of poems with familiar settings
Texts:	From *The Pain and the Great One,* Judy Blume
Resources:	Big Book 2A pp. 14–19 Pupil Book 2 pp. 8–9 Copymasters 1 and 4 Homework Book 2 p. 4

DAY 1

Big Book 2A pp. 14–15; Pupil Book 2 pp. 8–9

Shared reading

- Introduce the extract from *The Pain and the Great One* by Judy Blume, which begins on page 14 of Big Book 2A. Can the children remember reading another story by Judy Blume? (See Unit 2.)
- Read the Unit 3 title, *The Pain and the Great One,* which is also the title of the story by Judy Blume. Ask the class to read the subheading, *The Pain.* Explain that this is the title of the first half of the story. Can the children predict the title (*The Great One*) of the second half of the story?
- Read through the first page of the extract with the class.
- Who is telling this story? (Read the first line again: "My brother's a pain.")
- Discuss the things about her brother that annoy the narrator. Who carries "the Pain" into the kitchen for breakfast? Who helps him to get dressed?
- Read page 15 with the class. Discuss the things about her brother that annoy the narrator of this story. Refer to both the pages you have read with the children.
- Discuss whether the narrator is younger or older than her brother. Look for clues in the text.

Focused word/sentence work

- Talk about the way that the extract is set out in short lines like a poem.
- Discuss the style of the extract, which is written as though the child is listing her complaints aloud. Talk about the colloquialisms – everyday words – which have been used, e.g. *slowcoach, kid.*

Independent work

- The questions on page 9 of Pupil Book 2 relate to the extract from *The Pain and the Great One.*

Plenary

- Read pages 14 and 15 again with the class. Talk about the order of events in "the Pain's" typical day. Draw up a simple timetable to match the sequence of events described.

DAY 2

Big Book 2A pp. 14–16; Pupil Book 2 p. 9

Shared reading

- Re-read pages 14 and 15 with the class before reading page 16.
- Discuss the issue raised in the first paragraph on page 16. Do the children think that "the Pain" should be allowed to stay up as late as his older sister? Discuss why "the Pain" behaves as he does when his sister is on the phone.
- What is the "meanest thing of all"?

Focused word/sentence work

- Write the word *pain* on the board. Underline the rime *-ain.* Ask the children to suggest letters to replace the *p* to make new words, e.g. *brain, chain, drain, main, plain, rain, train, vain.*
- If the children suggest words with the same sound but a different spelling pattern, congratulate them for correctly recognising the long vowel sound and write the words in separate columns, e.g. *cane, crane, mane, plane.* Talk about the homophones, *plain/plane* and *main/mane.* Explain that they have the same sound but different meanings. Are the children able to tell you the different meanings?
- Write *ai* on the board. Ask the children to remind you of the other three vowels.

Independent work

- The first exercise for Days 2 and 3 on page 9 of Pupil Book 2 provides further practice of words containing the long vowel phoneme *ai.*

Plenary

- Explore a role-play situation based on the extract the children have read so far. In pairs, one child could play the older sister, the other, one of her parents. The sister could complain to the parent about the things Judy Blume has described in the extract. Encourage the children playing the parent to listen patiently and offer advice about how to deal with the annoying little brother. You may prefer to choose two confident children to explore the role-play situation in front of the whole class to stimulate a class discussion.

DAY 3

Big Book 2A pp. 16–18; Pupil Book 2 p. 9

Shared reading

- Introduce the second part of the extract, entitled "The Great One". Can the class predict who this section of the story will be about? Who will be telling it?
- Read pages 17 and 18 with the class. Discuss the little boy's feelings of jealousy towards his older sister. Talk about the things he is jealous of.
- Focus on the reference to feeding the cat on page 18. Turn back to page 16 to read "the Great One's" comments about the cat and discuss the two different viewpoints.

Focused word/sentence work

- Write *My sister thinks she's so great just because. . .* on the board. Ask different members of the class to read the sentence opener and complete it using examples from the text. Then ask the class to think of other ways to end the sentence using ideas of their own.

Independent work

- Exercise B on page 9 of Pupil Book 2 requires children to write about their own brother or sister. Encourage them to focus on the things they like about their brother or sister before writing about the things that they find annoying. Children with no siblings could write about the sort of brother or sister they would like to have.

Plenary

- Invite some of the children to read aloud their writing to the rest of the class.
- Look at the male/female names for different family members in the text: *brother/sister, Daddy/Mum*. Can the children tell you the male equivalent to the following: *aunty, gran, daughter, granddaughter*?

DAY 4

Pupil Book 2 p. 9; Copymaster 4

Shared writing

- Explain to the class that you are going to write a list of instructions, on behalf of "the Pain", entitled "How to Annoy Your Big Sister".
- Refer to the text, to pick out examples directly relating to the story, e.g. when your big sister is on the phone, dance around her, singing at the top of your voice.
- Encourage the class to think of other ideas of their own, e.g. borrow her things without asking; put plastic dinosaurs in her bed.
- Remind the class that this exercise is just for fun and they should not try any of these ideas out on older brothers and sisters at home!

Focused word/sentence work

- Once you have the best ideas in place, encourage the class to look at the structure of the writing. Check that every sentence begins with a capital letter and ends with a full stop. You may decide to number each instruction.

Independent work

- The children should begin writing their own set of instructions, on behalf of "the Pain", entitled "How to Annoy Your Big Sister", using Copymaster 4.

Plenary

- Ask the class to suggest ways that "the Pain" could *please* his older sister. Write down some of the best ideas, structuring the sentences in the same way as you did during the shared writing session.

DAY 5

Big Book 2A pp. 18–19; Pupil Book 2 p. 9; Copymaster 4 from Day 4

Shared reading

- Read pages 18 and 19 with the class.
- Why does "the Pain's" sister call him "baby"? How does he respond? What does "the Pain" do when his sister calls him a name? What do the children think he *should* do instead of hurting her? Why do Daddy and Mum yell at "the Pain"?
- Discuss the final line of this extract. Does the class think that Daddy and Mum love their daughter more than their son?

Focused word/sentence work

- Look at page 19. Can the children find a word with the *ai* sound as in "Pain" (*afraid*)?
- Focus on the word "pull". Listen to the short *oo* sound of the *u*. Write the word on the board and ask the children to think of a letter to replace the *p* with to make a word that means the opposite of empty (*full*). What initial letter would they use to make the name of an animal with horns (*bull*)?

Independent work

- The children complete the writing begun on Day 4.

Plenary

- Re-read sections of the extract. Ask the boys to read on behalf of "the Pain" while the girls read on behalf of "the Great One". Alternate between the two parts.

Consolidation and extension

- Read the full story of *The Pain and the Great One* by Judy Blume.
- Use Copymaster 1 to practise spelling words containing *ai*.

Homework

- Page 4 in Homework Book 2 requires children to write a set of instructions entitled, "How to Please Your Teacher".

Unit 4 Sorry Miss

Key Learning Objectives

TL6 to discuss familiar story themes and link to own experiences

TL11 to use language of time to structure a sequence of events, e.g. *when I had finished. . ., suddenly. . ., after that. . .*

WL2 to revise and extend the reading and spelling of words containing different spellings of the long vowel phonemes from Year 1

WL3 the common spelling patterns for the vowel phoneme *oo* (short as in *good*)

SL5 to revise knowledge about other uses of capitalisation, e.g. for names, headings, titles, emphasis, and begin to use in own writing

Range:	Fiction: stories with familiar settings
Texts:	From *Sorry Miss*, Jo Furtado
Resources:	Big Book 2A pp. 20–23 Pupil Book 2 pp. 10–11 Copymaster 5 Homework Book 2 p. 5

Preparation

- Day 5: prepare a set of word cards, large enough for the whole class to read, containing words with both sounds of *oo*, e.g. *book, cook, look, took; moon, school, soon, spoon.* You will also need a book and a spoon.

DAY 1

Big Book 2A pp. 20–21; Pupil Book 2 pp. 10–11

Shared reading

- Introduce this week's extract from *Sorry Miss* by Jo Furtado which begins on page 20 of Big Book 2A. Read through page 20 with the class. What is the child in the story apologising for? Who is he apologising to?
- Read through the second part of the extract on page 21. Why did the book get wet?
- Do the excuses sound genuine?

Focused word/sentence work

- Write the word *circus* on the board. Ask the children to read it to you. Underline the soft *c* in it. Can the children think of any other words with the soft *c* spelling? Give clues if necessary, e.g. *certain, circle.*
- Write the word *elephant* on the board. Ask the children to read it to you. Can they tell you what sound the *ph* is making?
- Write the word *gnome* on the board and ask the class to read it to you. Can they tell you which of the letters is silent?

Independent work

- The questions on page 11 of Pupil Book 2 relate to the first two pages of the extract from *Sorry Miss* by Jo Furtado.

Plenary

- Try a role-play situation using one of the storylines that the children have read today. Have one child playing the role of Miss Folio, and one playing the child who is offering the excuse.

DAY 2

Big Book 2A pp. 21–22; Pupil Book 2 p. 11

Shared reading

- Re-read page 21 with the children.
- Read page 22 with the children. Discuss the burglary that the child in the story describes. Do any of the children remember ever having something belonging to them taken by somebody else without permission? Encourage them to discuss how they felt about this.
- What things does the child in the story say were taken from his home? Where was the library book found? What does the child say happened to it?

Focused word/sentence work

- Can anyone think of another word that means the same as "burglar", e.g. *thief, robber*?
- Look at the words *policeman* and *fingerprints*. Show how each is made up of two smaller words. Cover the smaller words in turn to demonstrate this as a strategy for attempting to read unfamiliar words of this nature.
- Turn back to page 21. Ask a child to point out the words *book* and *good* on this page then write them on the board. Underline the short *oo* phoneme and demonstrate how it is pronounced. Remind the children of the long *oo* sound in words such as *food, moon* and *soon.* (Note that the pronunciation of the *oo* phoneme varies regionally; please adapt the work on *oo* in this unit as appropriate for your region.)

Independent work

- The exercise on page 11 of Pupil Book 2 focuses on the short *oo* phoneme, as in *book* and *good.*

Plenary

- Draw simple outlines of a book and a spoon on the board. Ask the class to help you label each drawing and underline *oo* in each. Say words containing *oo* aloud to the children and ask them to tell you whether the sound is short *oo* as in *book* or long *oo* as in *spoon.*

DAY 3

Big Book 2A pp. 22–23; Pupil Book 2 p. 11

Shared reading

- Re-read page 22 together.
- Read page 23 with the children. What do they think of this excuse?

Focused word/sentence work

- Find out if the children know what a "canal" is.
- Write the words *sorry* and *sky* on the board and underline the *y* in each. Ask the class to read these words to you and listen to the sound of the final *y*. Point to the word *smelly* and ask the children whether the *y* sound is the same as *y* in *sorry* or *sky*. Write the word *smelly* underneath *sorry* on the board. Repeat with the words *my* and *only*.

Independent work

- Use this time to complete the exercises on page 11 of Pupil Book 2.

Plenary

- Encourage the children to think up more excuses that could be used to explain why a library book is missing. Who can think of the most ridiculous excuse?

DAY 4

Pupil Book 2 p. 11; Copymaster 5

Shared writing

- Following on from the Plenary session on Day 3, read through the instruction for independent writing on page 11 of Pupil Book 2.
- Remind the children of some of the best excuses they offered for losing a library book and ask them to think of a good excuse for not having done their homework. Jot down some of the best suggestions on the board to make a bank of ideas for the children to refer to.
- Decide together on the best idea for a piece of shared writing. Write a sentence opener: *Sorry Miss Folio, I have not done my homework because . . .*
- Encourage the class to continue this sentence, using the idea you have already discussed together.

Focused word/sentence work

- Once you have established the main idea in your shared writing, expand on it, adding further details and embellishments to make the writing more interesting.
- Check together the sentence punctuation in your writing. Point out the capital letters in Miss Folio's name.
- Some children may have noticed the use of ellipsis in the original text. You may like to discuss the effect of this, but it is probably best to stick to conventional sentence punctuation when modelling writing at this stage.

Independent work

- Give each child a copy of Copymaster 5. Refer back to page 11 of Pupil Book 2 and ask the children to begin their own writing, using an idea already discussed as a class or another of their own.

Plenary

- Encourage the children to think of a range of excuses to finish sentences started by you, e.g. *Sorry, Mum, I have not tidied my room because . . .*
- The children might like to discuss times when they have made excuses in similar situations.

DAY 5

Big Book 2A pp. 20–23; Pupil Book 2 p. 11; Copymaster 5 from Day 4

Shared reading

- Re-read the whole of the extract on pages 20 to 23 with the class.
- Which, of all the excuses they have read this week, do the children think is the most far-fetched?

Focused word/sentence work

- Revise the different sounds of *oo* that the children have been focusing on this week. Give out cards with words containing the different sounds of *oo* in them. Ask two children to stand at the front of the class, one holding a book, the other holding a spoon. Ask the children with the word cards to come out, one at a time, and give their word to the child of the corresponding sound. When the task is complete, ask the children holding the props to show each card in turn and ask the class to read the words aloud to check that they are in the right set.

Independent work

- The children should use this time to complete the independent writing they began on Day 4.

Plenary

- Invite some of the children to read aloud their finished writing. Discuss the best features of their work. Discuss the use of any language of time that the children have used to structure the sequence of events, e.g. *When I had finished . . .; Suddenly . . .; After that . . .*

Consolidation and extension

- Read the full story of *Sorry Miss* by Jo Furtado.
- Ask the children to look for words containing short *oo* and *u* in their own reading books.

Homework

- Page 5 in Homework Book 2 requires children to write a story, based on a far-fetched excuse, to go with the pictures.

Unit 5

Granny's Quilt

Key Learning Objectives

TL4	to understand time and sequential relationships in stories
TL6	to discuss familiar story themes and link to own experiences
WL3	to learn the common spelling patterns for the vowel phonemes *ar* and *ow*
WL4	to investigate and classify words with the same sounds but different spellings
WL10	to learn new words from reading linked to particular topics, to build individual collections of personal interest or significant words
SL2	to find examples, in fiction and non-fiction, of words and phrases that link sentences, e.g. *after, meanwhile, during, before, then, next, after a while*
SL5	to revise knowledge about other uses of capitalisation, e.g. for names, headings, titles, emphasis, and begin to use in own writing

Range:	Fiction: stories with familiar settings
Texts:	From *Granny's Quilt*, Penny Ives
Resources:	Big Book 2A pp. 24–27 Pupil Book 2 pp. 12–13 Copymaster 6 Homework Book 2 p. 6

Preparation

- Day 5: prepare hexagons cut out of coloured paper on which children can write their sentences.

DAY 1

Big Book 2A pp. 24–25; Pupil Book 2. pp. 12–13

Shared reading

- Introduce the extract from *Granny's Quilt* which begins on page 24 of Big Book 2A. Read the first page together.
- Ask how many children have seen a patchwork quilt before.
- Read page 25. How many of the children have been to a christening? Ask them to talk about the occasion.

Focused word/sentence work

- Note the use of capital letters in both the unit heading and the title of the story extract.
- What are "hand-me-downs"?
- Talk about the motto, "make do and mend".
- Explain the meaning of the words "bloomers" and "frock".
- Point out the use of capital letters for names on page 25.

Independent work

- The questions on page 13 of Pupil Book 2 relate to today's extract from *Granny's Quilt*.

Plenary

- Write the word *patchwork* on the board. Show how it is made up of two smaller words by covering each in turn and asking the class to read the word that remains. See if they are able to think of words that rhyme with *patch* by changing the onset, e.g. *catch, hatch, latch, match, scratch*. Focus on the *-tch* ending of these words.

DAY 2

Big Book 2A pp. 25–26; Pupil Book 2 p. 13

Shared reading

- Re-read page 25 before reading page 26.

Focused word/sentence work

- Explain the meaning of the word "smock" on page 26.
- What is a "seam"? Ask the children to find a seam on their shirt or blouse.
- Focus on the words and phrases that show the order in which Granny's mother recycled the material with the pink flowers: *Then. . ., Next time round. . ., Finally. . . .*
- Read the final two sentences of page 26. Write the words *mouse* and *allowed* on the board and underline *ou* and *ow*. Read the words and draw the children's attention to the different spelling patterns of the *ou* phoneme. Can they think of other words containing this phoneme? Write their suggestions on the board under the word with the corresponding spelling pattern, e.g. *about, house, loud, out; cow, down, how, now.*

Independent work

- Exercise A on page 13 of Pupil Book 2 (Days 2 and 3) requires children to label different items of clothing.

Plenary

- Re-read pages 25 and 26 together.

DAY 3

Big Book 2A p. 27; Pupil Book 2 p. 13

Shared reading

- Read page 27 of Big Book 2A. What does a nanny do? Where did Granny meet Grandpa?

Focused word/sentence work

- Can the children find two exclamation marks on page 27? Talk about their function in these instances.
- Write the word *park* on the board and underline *ar*. Ask the children to read the word and then tell you the sound of the phoneme you have underlined. Give clues to other words containing the *ar* phoneme, e.g. *arm, art, dark, farm, garden, jar, party, star, start, shark.* As the children correctly guess each word, write it on the board and underline the *ar* phoneme.

Independent work

- Exercise B on page 13 of Pupil Book 2 (Days 2 and 3) requires children to make a list of the clothes they are wearing, describing the colours and material of each item.

Plenary

- Take another look at the illustrations throughout this unit. Discuss the style of the clothes.

DAY 4

Pupil Book 2 p. 13; Copymaster 6

Shared writing

- The writing on page 13 of Pupil Book 2 requires children to write about a special party or celebration that they remember. They are asked to make particular reference to the clothes they wore.
- Invite children to talk about a special occasion that they remember clearly. Decide upon a party or celebration to write about collectively. You may choose to write about a school event which all the children remember. Alternatively, you may choose one child to answer questions posed by the rest of the class about his or her celebration. Act as a scribe for the class.

Focused word/sentence work

- Discuss the organisation of the children's ideas as they have been presented. Help them re-structure the writing using simple sentences.
- Focus on the children's choice of vocabulary and look for ways to improve their descriptions.

Independent work

- The children may use this time to write about a party or celebration that they have attended. A writing frame is provided on Copymaster 6 to help children organise their writing.

Plenary

- Choose a few children to read their writing to the rest of the class. Discuss the best features of each.

DAY 5

Big Book 2A pp. 24–27; Pupil Book 2 p. 13; Copymaster 6 from Day 4

Shared reading

- Re-read the entire extract on pages 24 to 27 together.

Focused word/sentence work

- Look at the titles of the family members mentioned in the story: *Granny/Grandpa*; *brothers/sisters*; *Mother*. Do any of the children have different names for their grandparents, e.g. *Gran, Grandmother, Nan, Nana, Nanny; Grampy, Grandad, Grandfather*?

Independent work

- Use this time for the completion of the children's writing from Day 4.

Plenary

- Choose different children to read their completed writing. Invite the rest of the class to ask questions relating to the event they have heard described.

Consolidation and extension

- Give each child a hexagon cut out of coloured paper. Ask them to write a couple of sentences about a special memory on their hexagon. Assemble the hexagons on a wall display to make a "patchwork quilt".
- Invite the children to bring in photographs of special events and tell their classmates about the occasions.
- Make a collection of photographs and pictures of clothing from different periods. Construct a timeline to show the order in which each type of clothing was fashionable.

Homework

- Page 6 of Homework Book 2 provides children with an opportunity to write another special memory.

Unit 6

Tall Inside

Key Learning Objectives

TL5	to identify and discuss reasons for events in stories, linked to plot
TL6	to discuss familiar story themes and link to own experiences
TL10	to use story structure to write about own experience in same/similar form
WL1	to secure identification, spelling and reading of long vowel digraphs in simple words
WL2	to revise and extend the reading and spelling of words containing different spellings of the long vowel phonemes from Year 1
WL3	the common spelling patterns for the vowel phonemes *oy* and *ow*
WL4	to investigate and classify words with the same sounds but different spellings
WL7	to use word endings, e.g. *-ing* (present tense) to support reading and spelling
SL5	to revise knowledge about other uses of capitalisation, e.g. for names, headings, titles, emphasis, and begin to use in own writing

Range:	Fiction and poetry: stories and a variety of poems with familiar settings
Texts:	From *Tall Inside*, Jean Richardson
Resources:	Big Book 2A pp. 28–35 Pupil Book 2 pp. 14–15 Copymaster 1 Homework Book 2 p. 7

Preparation

- Days 3 and 4: you will need cards with some of the following words written on them: *borrow, crow, follow, grow, know, slow, snow, throw, window, yellow; brown, crowd, down, flower, frown, how, now, owl, town, vowel.*

DAY 1

Big Book 2A pp. 28–30; Pupil Book 2 pp. 14–15

Shared reading

- Introduce the extract from *Tall Inside* by Jean Richardson. Read through pages 28 to 30 with the class.
- What can Joanne do that Rosie cannot? What do the children think about Rosie's rule for joining the club? Why was Jo upset?
- It says in the story that Humpty "was used to getting wet". What does this suggest?

Focused word/sentence work

- What is the name of Joanne's brother? What is the name of her best friend? What is Joanne's bear called? Ask a volunteer to point to these names. What do the children notice about them? Where else on these pages are capital letters used (title, beginning of sentences, other names).
- Can the children find a question mark on page 30? Who is asking the question?

Independent work

- The comprehension questions on page 15 of Pupil Book 2 relate to today's extract from *Tall Inside* by Jean Richardson.

Plenary

- Encourage the children to discuss occasions when people have been unkind to them. Perhaps other children have called them names because of the way they look. Invite them to discuss how they felt (without mentioning the names of other children involved!).

DAY 2

Big Book 2A pp. 30–32; Pupil Book 2 p. 15

Shared reading

- Re-read page 30 to remind the children of the story extract so far. Ask them to tell you what happened between Jo, Jenny and her cousins.
- Read through page 31 together. Ask the class to describe the clown to you.
- Read page 32 with the class. Why did Lofty not notice Jo at first?

Focused word/sentence work

- Can the children suggest why "**Please can I help?**" is printed in bold type?
- Write the following sentence on the board: *Lofty invited the children to join him in the ring.* Ask the class to read the sentence to you. Then ask them to say aloud the sound that you have underlined.
- Write *oi* on the board and ask the class to think of words containing this spelling pattern. Give clues to words containing the sound *oi*, e.g. *boil, coin, join, noise, point, poison, spoil, toilet.* Write each word on the board.
- Write *oy* on the board and explain that this spelling pattern sounds the same as *oi*. Give clues to words containing the *oy* spelling pattern e.g. *annoy, boy, destroy, enjoy, joy, toy.* Write each word on the board.

Independent work

- The exercises for Days 2 and 3 on page 15 of Pupil Book 2 focus on the use of capital letters for names, and on words containing *oi* and *oy*.

Plenary

- Look at some of the words on pages 30 and 31 that tell us what different characters were doing: *laughing, clapping* and *juggling.* Write these words on the board and underline *ing* in each. Can the children find any other words ending in *-ing* on page 31 (*trying, catching*)?
- Invite individual children to mime these and other words ending in *-ing*. Whoever guesses the word correctly performs the next mime.

DAY 3

Big Book 2A pp. 32–34; Pupil Book 2 p. 15

Shared reading

- Ask the class to re-tell the story they have read so far.
- Read pages 32 and 33 with the class. Find out how many of the children can do a somersault, a cartwheel or a handstand.
- Read page 34. How many children have seen someone walking on stilts?

Focused word/sentence work

- Draw the children's attention to the compound words on page 33: *greasepaint, upturned, cartwheels* and *handstand*. Ask the class to read the words aloud. Can they identify the two smaller words in each?
- Write the word *clown* on the board and underline *ow*. Ask the class to read the word and then say aloud the underlined phoneme. Challenge the children to think of letters to replace the consonant cluster *cl* to make new words, e.g. *brown, down, frown, gown, town*. Offer clues to these words, e.g. *What is the opposite of up?* and ask the children to tell you the letters that would be needed to replace *cl*.

Independent work

- Children should use this time to complete the exercises on page 15 of Pupil Book 2.

Plenary

- Write the words *clown* and *show* on the board. Read the words aloud and compare the sound of the *ow* phonemes. Hand out word cards with words containing *ow* to different children (see **Preparation**). Ask them to read each word aloud and decide whether the sound of the *ow* phoneme is the same as *ow* in *clown* or *show*. You may like to invite the children to write their word on the board under the word with the corresponding sound.

DAY 4

Pupil Book 2 p. 15

Shared writing

- Using evidence from this week's text, help the children to write a few sentences describing the things that made Joanne feel sad: feeling different from her friends because she was shorter than them, feeling left out. Explain how these things made Jo feel.
- Now ask the children to think of times that others were unkind to them. Without giving names, ask the children to give examples of the things that people have been unkind about and write these on the board, e.g. name calling, leaving someone out of a game, telling lies about someone, making fun of the way a person looks, laughing when someone makes a mistake.

Focused word/sentence work

- Discuss with the children the task that is outlined on page 15 of Pupil Book 2. Consider different ways of beginning the writing, using the children's ideas. Decide on a sentence opener together and write it on the board. Perhaps someone would be willing to continue the sentence with an example from their own experience, e.g. *I felt sad when one of my friends was having a party and I wasn't invited.*
- Discuss how to develop the writing further.

Independent work

- Ask each child to complete the writing task set out on page 15 of Pupil Book 2 using an example from his or her own experience.

Plenary

- Repeat the game played during the plenary session on Day 3, using the *ow* word cards.

DAY 5

Big Book 2A pp. 35

Shared reading

- Re-read page 34 before reading page 35 with the class. Discuss Lofty's final words about feeling "tall inside". What does he mean by this?

Focused word/sentence work

- Can the children find a word on page 35 which contains the sound *ow* as in *show* (*growing*)? Can they find a word which contains the sound *ow* as in *clown* (*down*)?
- Turn back to page 34. Can the children find another word which contains the sound *ow* as in *clown* (*towered*)?
- Read page 34 again with the children and ask them to look out for three words which contain the sound *ow* as in *clown*, but with a different spelling pattern (*outfit, round, trousers*).

Independent work

- Complete the independent writing activity started on Day 4.

Plenary

- Role-play a few different playground situations with the children, exploring different themes, e.g. a child being left out of a game.

Consolidation and extension

- Use Copymaster 1 to practise spelling the vowel phonemes *oy, oi, ow* or *ou*.

Homework

- Page 7 in Homework Book 2 focuses on the different sounds of *ow* as in *clown* and *snowman*.

Unit 7 Snowy

Key Learning Objectives

TL5	to identify and discuss reasons for events in stories, linked to plot
TL6	to discuss familiar story themes and link to own experiences
WL3	the common spelling patterns for the vowel phoneme *ar*
WL10	learn new words from reading linked to particular topics, to build individual collections of personal interest or significant words

Range:	Fiction and poetry: stories and a variety of poems with familiar settings.
Texts:	From *Snowy*, Berlie Doherty, Collins
Resources:	Big Book 2A pp. 36–44 Pupil Book 2 pp. 16–17 Copymaster 1 Homework Book 2 p. 8

Preparation

- Days 1 and 2: prepare a set of cards featuring words containing *ar*, e.g. *arm, art, bark, car, dark, farm, garden, hard, jar, party, shark, star, start.*

DAY 1

Big Book 2A pp. 36–37; Pupil Book 2 pp. 16–17

Shared reading

- Introduce the extract from *Snowy* by Berlie Doherty. Can the children remember reading anything else written by Berlie Doherty (*The Magical Bicycle*, Unit 1)?
- Read through page 36 with the class. How many children have seen a barge, or narrowboat? Can they tell you how a canal is different from an ordinary river? Ask the children to describe the way Rachel's narrowboat is decorated.
- Read page 37. What does Rachel call the narrowboat? What does she love best about it? What is Snowy's job?

Focused word/sentence work

- Point to the words *slish! slosh!* on page 36. Read them together and ask the children to tell you what they notice. Can they find a similar pair of words on page 37 (*splish! splash!*)?
- Write the word *barge* on the board and underline *ar*. Ask the class to read aloud the sound you have underlined.
- Hand out a set of word cards with words containing *ar* (see **Preparation**) to different children. Ask each child in turn to give a clue to their *ar* word (some may need help reading their word), e.g. a noise that a dog makes. As each word is guessed correctly, write it on the board.

Independent work

- The questions on page 17 of Pupil Book 2 relate to today's extract from *Snowy*.

Plenary

- Talk about what it would be like to live on a narrowboat. What would the children like best about it? What would they miss?

DAY 2

Big Book 2A pp. 38–40; Pupil Book 2 p. 17

Shared reading

- Read the last sentence on page 37 before reading through pages 38 to 40 together. Why wouldn't Rachel's mum let her take Snowy to school? What is Snowy's "work"? What pets did the other children bring into school? Does anyone in the class own any of these pets? If they could have any pet they liked, what would they choose for themselves?

Focused word/sentence work

- Revise the *ar* vowel phoneme by playing the game that you played on Day 1, using the word cards.
- Can the children find a word on page 39, containing *ar* (*cardigan*)?

Independent work

- Exercise A on page 17 of Pupil Book 2 focuses on the vowel phoneme *ar*.

Plenary

- Re-read pages 38 to 40 with the class.

DAY 3

Big Book 2A pp. 41–43; Pupil Book 2 p. 17

Shared reading

- Ask the children to remind you about why Rachel was feeling upset. Read pages 41 to 43 together. Talk about Rachel's surprise. What do the children think prompted Rachel's teacher to plan the surpise? Discuss how Rachel would probably feel about it.
- Invite the children to point out the feathers around Snowy's hooves, her bells and her shining brasses in the illustration.

Focused word/sentence work

- Write the word *barge* on the board. Ask the children to think of names of other places where people live, e.g. *bungalow, castle, flat, house, palace, lighthouse*. Write these names on the board. Ask the children to talk about the different features, good and bad, of each type of home. Find out where they would most like to live and ask them to give reasons for their choices. You may like to conduct a class survey which could be made into a block graph at a later date.

Independent work

- Once the children have completed exercise A on page 17 of Pupil Book 2, ask them to match the labels to the different types of housing shown in exercise B.

Plenary

- Re-read pages 41 and 42.

- Look at some of the compound words on pages 41 and 42: *haystacks, afternoon, outside, everybody*. Cover, in turn, the smaller words within each compound word. Show how this can be used as a reading strategy. Talk about the way the meaning of a word made up of two smaller words can be found by thinking about the meaning of the smaller words, e.g. a haystack is a stack of hay.

DAY 4

Pupil Book 2 p. 17

Shared writing

- Introduce the writing task outlined on page 17 of Pupil Book 2. Choose an example of somewhere the children would like to live (perhaps their most popular choice of home discussed on Day 3).
- Make a list of reasons for wanting to live in such a place.
- Can the children think of any disadvantages?

Focused word/sentence work

- Help the children transfer their ideas from the lists you have made into a cohesive piece of writing.
- Check the punctuation of the writing together and discuss whether anything could be improved.

Independent work

- The children should write about the place where they would most like to live, explaining why they would like to live there and how it would be different from where they currently live.

Plenary

- Invite children to read out their writing. Ask the class to suggest what else might be included in each piece of writing.

DAY 5

Big Book 2A pp. 37–38, 43–44

Shared reading

- Read the final two pages of the extract from *Snowy*. Talk about the success of Rachel's teacher's plan. What did Rachel's friends say about Snowy?
- Focus on the last sentence of the extract on page 44. Does it sound familiar to the children? Turn back to page 38 to find the simile, "like a painted swan". Compare the words *floats* (page 38) and *glide* (page 44). What other similarities are there in the last sentence on page 37 and the first on page 38 with the last sentence on page 43 and the first on page 44? ("When Mum clicks her tongue and says, 'Come on Snowy,' she lowers her head . . . she plod, plod, plods."/"Mum clicked her tongue. 'Come on Snowy,' she said. Snowy lowered her head and began to . . . plod, plod, plod.")

Focused word/sentence work

- Challenge the children to find the names of five different parts of the body on pages 43 and 44 (*mouths, tooth, tongue, head, hand*). Acknowledge the very irregular spelling of the word *tongue*.
- Talk in general about Berlie Doherty's descriptions of the narrowboat and Snowy. Which descriptive lines do the children like best?

Independent work

- Ask the children to complete the writing task started on Day 4.

Plenary

- Invite some of the children to read aloud their writing to the rest of the class. Choose children who have written about different places.

Consolidation and extension

- Read the full version of *Snowy* by Berlie Doherty.
- Use Copymaster 1 to practise spelling words containing the *ar* vowel phoneme.
- Make a class book about different types of housing or different pets.

Homework

- Page 8 in Homework Book 2 requires children to write the names of pets and sentences about a pet.

Unit 8

A Worm's Eye View

Key Learning Objectives

TL3	to be aware of the difference between spoken and written language through comparing oral recounts with text; make use of formal story elements in re-telling
TL4	to understand time and sequential relationships in stories
TL5	to identify and discuss reasons for events in stories, linked to plot
TL6	to discuss familiar story themes and link to own experiences, e.g. illness, getting lost, going away
TL10	to use story structure to write about own experience in same/similar form
WL3	the common spelling patterns for the vowel phoneme *ow*
WL4	to investigate and classify words with the same sounds but different spellings
WL7	to use word endings, e.g. *-s* (plural), *-ed* (past tense), *-ing* (present tense) to support reading and spelling
SL2	to find examples, in fiction and non-fiction, of words and phrases that link sentences, e.g. *after, meanwhile, during, before, then, next, after* a *while*
SL3	to recognise and take account of commas and exclamation marks in reading aloud with appropriate expression

Range:	Fiction: stories with familiar settings
Texts:	From *A Worm's Eye View*, Jan Mark
Resources:	Big Book 2A pp. 45–52 Pupil Book 2 pp. 18–19 Homework Book 2 p. 9

Preparation

- Day 1: prepare a set of word cards featuring the following verbs: *jump, shout, walk,* and *crawl.*
- Day 2: you will need illustrated dictionaries (one for each pair).

DAY 1

Big Book 2A pp. 45–49; Pupil Book 2 pp. 18–19

Shared reading

- Introduce the extract from *A Worm's Eye View* by Jan Mark.
- Read pages 45 to 46 with the class. What is an allotment?
- What relation is David to Alice and Tom? What did they use to transport the tools in? What did David do when he was allowed out of the buggy?
- Read pages 47 to 49.

Focused word/sentence work

- Re-read the following sentences on page 45: "Tom pushed an old pram with the small tools in it. Alice pushed their cousin David in the buggy."
- Write the word *pushed* on the board and underline *ed.* Talk about this word ending and how it shows that the action took place in the past.
- Look at pages 45 and 46 together. Ask the children to find more words that end in *-ed* (*reached, growled, stamped, squashed, parked*). Write these words on the board and underline *-ed* in each one.
- Ask a volunteer to pretend that they are David, growling and stamping on the nice grass. Write the following sentence on the board to show that it is happening now: *(Name) is growling and stamping on the nice grass.* Underline *-ing* in these words.

Independent work

- The questions on page 19 of Pupil Book 2 relate to today's extract from *A Worm's Eye View* by Jan Mark.

Plenary

- Using a set of action word cards (see **Preparation**) ask a volunteer to take a card, read it, and perform the action to the class. Once the mimed action word, e.g. *jump,* has been correctly guessed, ask the child to repeat the mime while you write (*Name*) *is jumping* on the board. Whoever guessed the mime correctly takes the next card. At the end of the game ask the children to tell you, in the correct order, who did what. Record the information as follows, e.g. *Richard jumped, Pepe walked, Annie shouted and Theo crawled.* Compare these verb endings (*-ed*) with those in the previous sentences (*-ing*).

DAY 2

Big Book 2A pp. 45–49; Pupil Book 2 p. 19

Shared reading

- Re-read pages 45 to 49 with the class.
- Discuss with the class whether they think Tom and Alice like looking after their young cousin.

Focused word/sentence work

- Re-read the very first sentence of the extract: "The allotments were behind the house, at the end of the garden." Point to the word *house* and ask the children to read it to you. Underline the *ou* vowel phoneme and ask the children to say the sound. Can they think of a small creature that rhymes with *house* (*mouse*)?
- Turn to page 48 and read the second to last sentence together. Write the word *round* on the board. Can the children think of letters to put in place of the letter *r* to make new words, e.g. *found, ground, hound, mound, pound, sound*? If they suggest an inappropriate letter, try it anyway to make a nonsense word for the children to enjoy reading aloud.
- Turn back to page 47. Read the first sentence to the class: "Alice took the trowel out of the pram and gave it to David."
- Ask the children to look for a word containing the *ou* sound. Write the word *trowel* on the board and underline *ow.* Discuss how the spelling pattern *ow* sometimes sounds the same as *ou.* Write down a few examples, e.g. *brown, cow, down, how, town.*

Independent work

- The exercises on page 19 of Pupil Book 2 for Day 2 focus on *ou* (as in *mouse*) and *ow* (as in *clown*).

Plenary

- Hand out illustrated dictionaries to the children (one for each pair). Challenge the children to look up words that you call out and find out whether the word contains *ou* or *ow*. See who can be the first to locate each word by its initial sound, e.g. *clown, flower, house, mouse, mouth, town*. Write each word on the board once it has been found and underline *ou* or *ow*.

DAY 3

Big Book 2A pp. 49–51; Pupil Book 2 p. 19

Shared reading

- Re-read the last two sentences of page 48 before moving on to read pages 49 to 51.
- Ask the children to think about what will happen next.

Focused word/sentence work

- What is a compost heap?
- Choose four children to read the words spoken by Dad, Tom, Mum and David. Re-read the last sentence of page 49 and pages 50 to 51 with the class reading the narration. Talk about the function of the speech marks in indicating which lines are spoken by each character.

Independent work

- The children should use this time to complete the exercises on page 19 of Pupil Book 2.

Plenary

- Read through the last sentence of page 49 and pages 50 to 51, with four different children reading the words spoken by Dad, Tom, Mum and David.

DAY 4

Pupil Book 2 p. 19

Shared writing

- Read together the writing challenge on page 19 of Pupil Book 2: "Imagine what would happen if Alice and Tom took David to the supermarket. Write a story about the things that David might do."
- Ask the children to make suggestions about the sorts of things that could go wrong, e.g. David knocking down a display of baked beans, wandering away and getting lost, or going through doors marked "NO ENTRY". Encourage the children to discuss their most memorable visits to supermarkets.
- Help the children to structure a simple story using their ideas. Discuss the story in terms of beginning (introducing characters and setting), middle (main action) and end (conclusion).

Focused word/sentence work

- Once you have established the structure, help the class look for opportunities to improve their writing. Check the sentence punctuation together. Encourage the children to introduce new vocabulary to their writing.

Independent work

- Ask the children to begin writing a story using their own ideas or those that were developed during the shared writing session. Remind them that they should begin by introducing the characters and describing the supermarket setting before writing about all the things that go on. Explain that time will be given on Day 5 to complete the stories.

Plenary

- Invite a few children to read their stories so far. Discuss the best features and encourage the class to look for ways to improve each piece of writing. You may find it useful to refer back to the shared writing.

DAY 5

Big Book 2A pp. 51–52

Shared reading

- Re-read page 51 before moving on to read the conclusion to this week's extract by Jan Mark.
- What do the children think about the way the story ends? Did it end in the way they had predicted it would?

Focused word/sentence work

- Look at the two question words on page 51: *which* and *where*. Ask the children to think of other words which can be used to begin a question, e.g. *when, why, how*. Ask them to think of a question, beginning with each of these words, to ask the rest of the class.
- Look at the word *climb* on page 52. Which letter in this word is silent?

Independent work

- The children should use this time to finish the stories they began on Day 4.

Plenary

- Invite different children to read their completed stories. Discuss the best features of each.

Consolidation and extension

- Read the extended story of *A Worm's Eye View* by Jan Mark in its entirety.

Homework

- Page 9 in Homework Book 2 focuses on making words with the *ou* sound as in *shout*.

Unit 9

Home Grown

Key Learning Objectives

TL13 to read simple written instructions in the classroom, simple recipes, plans, instructions for constructing something

TL14 to note key structural features, e.g. clear statement of purpose at start, sequential steps set out in a list, direct language

TL15 to write simple instructions

TL16 to use models from reading to organise instructions sequentially, e.g. listing points in order, each point depending on the previous one, numbering

TL17 to use diagrams in instructions, e.g. drawing and labelling diagrams as part of a set of instructions

TL18 to use appropriate register in writing instructions, i.e. direct, impersonal, building on texts read

SL6 to use a variety of simple organisational devices, e.g. arrows, lines, boxes, keys, to indicate sequences and relationships

Range:	Non-fiction: instructions
Texts:	From *Kitchen Fun*, Ray Gibson *Making a Christmas Tree*
Resources:	Big Book 2A pp. 53–56 Pupil Book 2 pp. 20–21 Copymaster 7 Homework Book 2 p. 10

Preparation

- Day 1: have some cress seeds, cotton wool and felt ready to show the children.
- Day 3: have ready all the resources listed on page 56 of Big Book 2A for a demonstration.

DAY 1

Big Book 2A pp. 53-54

Shared reading

- Introduce *Cress Creatures – Woolly Sheep* from *Kitchen Fun* by Ray Gibson. What sort of writing is it?
- Read through the list of items under the heading "You will need".
- Show the children some cress seeds, cotton wool and felt.
- Read through the first four instructions.
- What is used to make the body of the sheep? What are the sheep's legs made of?

Focused word/sentence work

- Look at some of the features of instructional writing. Discuss why it is necessary to list the resources needed and why the list appears at the beginning. Why are the instructions numbered? Look at the action words, *Pull*, *Cut* and *Add* which begin the instructions.

Independent work

- The questions on page 21 of Pupil Book 2 relate to the extract, *Cress Creatures – Woolly Sheep*.

Plenary

- Read through the list of items under the heading "You will need" again, then close the book. See how many of the different items the children are able to recall.

DAY 2

Big Book 2A pp. 53–55; Pupil Book 2 pp. 20–21

Shared reading

- Read through the seven instructions which begin on page 53 and end on page 55 of Big Book 2A.
- Talk about the finished product that would be made if the instructions were followed. Would it be useful? Would it be nice to look at?
- Have any of the children grown cress before? What did they serve it with? How did it taste?
- Why is it necessary to keep the cotton wool wet?
- Would it matter if you were to try to follow the instructions in a different order?

Focused word/sentence work

- Can anyone tell you what "fleece" is? What does "shear" mean? (Refer to the context of the word which provides a clue to its meaning: "to shear with scissors".) Can the children tell you what a sheep's fleece is used for when it is shorn?
- Ask the children to give you instructions, orally, on how to wash your hair. Write down exactly what they tell you and then evaluate the instructions together.

Independent work

- The first activity on page 21 of Pupil Book 2 requires the children to sequence a set of instructions on how to wash your hair.

Plenary

- Look at the words *First of all*, *Then* and *Finally*, used to begin instructions on page 21 of Pupil Book 2. Discuss how each of these words gives a clue to the sequence of the instructions, e.g. *First of all* could not be used anywhere other than at the beginning of the first instruction, whereas *Then* suggests something has already taken place.

DAY 3

Big Book 2A p. 56; Pupil Book 2 p. 21

Shared reading

- Read the title *Making a Christmas Tree* on page 56 of Big Book 2A. Does it explain the purpose of the instructions that follow? Talk about how the title is a statement of purpose. Read the instructions together. Discuss the importance of the pictures in showing where to make cuts, and how to put the trees together etc.

Focused word/sentence work

- Look again at some of the features of instructional writing. Look at the action words, *cut*, *colour* and *decorate*. Talk about the usefulness of the illustrations. How easy would it be to construct the model without the pictures?

Independent work

- Exercise B on page 21 of Pupil Book 2 requires children to sequence a set of bedtime tasks. Remind the children that their own order of tasks may be different from their friends'.

Plenary

- Choose one or two children to help you with a demonstration. Ask the rest of the class to read the instructions on page 56 of Big Book 2A aloud as you demonstrate how to construct the Christmas tree.

DAY 4

Pupil Book 2 p. 21; Copymaster 7

Shared writing

- Read through the writing task outlined on page 21 of Pupil Book 2.
- Begin by making a list of the different things you would expect to find in a hamster cage: e.g. sawdust, bedding material, food dish, water bottle.
- Ask the children to think about and describe the different stages involved in cleaning out a hamster cage. Write down each step as it is described to you. Encourage the class to discuss each contribution that is made.

Focused word/sentence work

- Look closely at the order in which the instructions have been written. Once the children are happy with the sequencing, number each step.
- Check the punctuation together.
- Can any of the steps be simplified or written in a clearer way? Discuss your ideas with the class and encourage them to review their combined work and redraft as necessary.

Independent work

- Copymaster 7 may be used to assist the children in writing instructions for cleaning out a hamster cage. More able children might prefer to structure their writing in their own way without the use of the writing frame.

Plenary

- Invite a few children to read their writing so far. Discuss the best features of each and encourage the class to offer help where instructions have become muddled.

DAY 5

Big Book 2A p. 56; Pupil Book 2 p. 21; Copymaster 7 from Day 4

Shared reading

- Read page 56 with the class once more.

Focused word/sentence work

- Close the book and see if the children can recall the resources needed to make the Chrstmas tree model. Write down the items they remember. Then ask the class to tell you each instruction in turn from memory. Write down the steps that they tell you. Open Big Book 2A at page 56 once more and compare the instructions there with those that the children gave you. How well did they remember the instructions? What differences are there?

Independent work

- The children should use this time to complete the instructional writing they began on Day 4.

Plenary

- Invite a few of the children to read out their instructions. Discuss whether they have presented the different steps involved in cleaning out a hamster cage in a logical order.

Consolidation and extension

- The children would enjoy following the instructions on pages 53 to 55 of Big Book 2A to make their own cress creature.

Homework

- Using the instructions on page 10 of Homework Book 2, the children can make their own Christmas tree.

Unit 10 Josie Smith at Christmas

Key Learning Objectives

TL3 to be aware of the difference between spoken and written language through comparing oral recounts with text; make use of formal story elements in re-telling

TL4 to understand time and sequential relationships in stories

TL5 to identify and discuss reasons for events in stories, linked to plot

TL13 to read simple written instructions in the classroom, simple recipes, plans, instructions for constructing something

TL14 to note key structural features, e.g. clear statement of purpose at start, sequential steps set out in a list, direct language

TL16 to use models from reading to organise instructions sequentially, e.g. listing points in order, each point depending on the previous one, numbering

TL18 to use appropriate register in writing instructions, i.e. direct, impersonal, building on texts read

WL7 to use word endings, e.g. *-ed* (past tense), to support reading and spelling

SL2 to find examples, in fiction and non-fiction, of words and phrases that link sentences, e.g. *after, meanwhile, during, before, then, next, after a while*

SL3 to recognise and take account of commas and exclamation marks in reading aloud with appropriate expression

SL5 to revise knowledge about other uses of capitalisation, e.g. for names, headings, titles, emphasis, and begin to use in own writing

Range:	Fiction: stories with familiar settings Non-fiction: instructions
Texts:	From *Josie Smith at Christmas*, Magdalen Nabb, Collins
Resources:	Big Book 2A pp. 57–64 Pupil Book 2 pp. 22–23 Copymasters 8–9 Assessment master, Term 1 Homework Book 2 p. 11

DAY 1

Big Book 2A pp. 57–59; Pupil Book 2 pp. 22–23

Shared reading

- Read the first page of the extract from *Josie Smith at Christmas*, by Magdalen Nabb, which begins on page 57 of Big Book 2A. At what time of year is the story set?
- Read pages 58 and 59. What do the children think of Eileen? What do the children think of Miss Potts?

Focused word/sentence work

- Read through the final paragraphs on page 58 once more together. How many words ending in *-ed* can the children find? Write these words on the board and underline *ed* in each: *started, pushed, shoved, crashed, banged, shouted, argued, scraped, bumped, opened, marched.* Talk about the function of *-ed* in these words.

Independent work

- There are questions to test the children's comprehension of today's fiction extract on page 23 of Pupil Book 2.

Plenary

- Refer to the words you wrote on the board during today's focused word/sentence work. Read each word in turn to the children in the past tense and ask them to respond by telling you what the word would be in the present tense, e.g. *started/start.* As the children tell you what each word would be in the present tense, rub out *ed.* Draw the children's attention to the fact that you are only removing the letter *d* from the words *shoved, argued,* and *scraped.* Can they tell you why this is?

DAY 2

Big Book 2A pp. 58–61; Pupil Book 2 p. 23

Shared reading

- Re-read the final two sentences of page 58 before re-reading page 59.
- Now move on to read pages 60 and 61. Do the children feel sorry for Gary? What do they think Miss Valentine will do about the broken angel?

Focused word/sentence work

- Can the children find three words that end in *ed* on page 59 (*stopped, frightened, roared*)?
- Write a selection of verbs on the board, e.g. *jump, pull, walk, shout.* Ask the children to read each word in turn and tell you what it would be in the past tense (by adding *-ed*).
- Talk about the use of exclamation marks on page 59. How should the sentences that end with an exclamation mark be read?

Independent work

- Exercise A on page 23 of Pupil Book 2 (Days 2 and 3) reinforces the verb ending *-ed*.

Plenary

- Re-read today's extract from *Josie Smith at Christmas*.

DAY 3

Big Book 2A pp. 62–64; Pupil Book 2 p. 23

Shared reading

- Read pages 62 to 64. Talk about the materials and method Josie Smith uses to make her angel. Why do the children think Josie is making an angel?

Focused word/sentence work

- Re-read the description of Josie Smith making an angel on pages 63 and 64, and pick out the items that Josie uses to make her angel. List these on the board.

Independent work

- Exercise B on page 23 of Pupil Book 2 requires the children to write a few sentences of their own using verbs ending in *-ed*.

Plenary

- Look at the different steps involved in making the angel on pages 63 and 64. List these steps on a board or flip chart as though compiling a set of instructions. Number each "instruction" and use terms common to instructional text, e.g. *first, then, next*. Note the change of tense, emphasising that stories are usually written in the past tense.

DAY 4

Big Book 2A p. 57; Pupil Book 2 p. 23

Shared writing

- On page 23 of Pupil Book 2 the children are asked to write a short story about Josie Smith's class. They are to imagine that someone has broken a window during playtime and write about Miss Pott's reaction to this.
- You may like to refer back to the opening paragraph on page 57, to reflect upon the setting described by Magdalen Nabb.
- Help the children to write an opening paragraph introducing the setting and main characters.
- Help the class develop their writing using the suggested storyline. Discuss how the story will end. Will someone own up to the accident or will somebody else report the culprit to Miss Potts? What will she have to say about it?

Focused word/sentence work

- Re-read the shared writing and help the class re-draft as appropriate. Is the writing in keeping with Magdalen Nabb's story extract?

Independent work

- The children may now begin writing their own Josie Smith story, using ideas developed collectively during the shared writing session. Remind the children to use capital letters for names; write the names of the main characters from the story extract on the board for the class to refer to.

Plenary

- Invite a few of the children to read their writing to the rest of the class. Discuss any new ideas which these children have introduced into their writing.

DAY 5

Big Book 2A pp. 57–64

Shared reading

- Re-read pages 57 to 61.

Focused word/sentence work

- Focus once more on the words ending in *-ed* on page 57. Point to each word in turn and ask the children to tell you what it would be without its *-ed* ending.

Independent work

- The children may use this time to finish their story writing.

Plenary

- Re-read the description of Josie Smith making her angel on pages 62 to 64.

Consolidation and extension

- Copymaster 8 provides instructions on how to make a paper angel using the template on Copymaster 9.
- Read more about Josie Smith from one of the collections of stories about her by Magdalen Nabb.
- The Assessment master for Term 1 provides revision of teaching points covered this term as a means of assessing children's progress.

Homework

- Page 11 of Homework Book 2 provides a writing frame for the children to write an imaginary letter from the headmistress, Miss Potts, to the parents of Gary Grimes, explaining his recent misdemeanour.

TERM 2

HALF-TERMLY PLANNER

Year 2 • Term 2 • Weeks 1–5

SCHOOL ________________ **CLASS** ________ **TEACHER** ____________

		Phonetics, spelling and vocabulary	Grammar and punctuation	Comprehension and composition	Texts
Continuous work **Weeks 1–5**		WL 6, 7, 9, 12, 13 14	SL 1, 2, 3, 4, 9	TL 1, 2, 12	**Range** **Fiction and poetry:** traditional stories: stories and poems from other cultures; stories and poems with predictable and patterned language; poems by significant children's poets **Non-fiction:** (i) dictionaries, glossaries, indexes (ii) explanations
Blocked work **Week**	**Unit**				**Titles**
1	11	WL 3	SL 6	TL 3, 4, 6, 7	From *The Story of the Frog Prince*, retold by Margaret Carter; From *The Princess and the Pig* in *The Triffic Pig Book*, Dick King-Smith
2	12	WL 10, 11	SL 7	TL 16, 17, 18	From *All Pigs are Beautiful*, Dick King-Smith
3	13	WL 2	SL 5	TL 4, 6, 7	From *Dog, Cat and Monkey* in *The Children's Book of Animal Stories*, ed. Michael Rosen
4	14	WL 2, 10	SL 8	TL 8, 9, 10, 11, 15	*Chips*, Stanley Cook; *Spaghetti! Spaghetti!*, Jack Prelutsky; *Hot Food*, Michael Rosen; *Chapatti in Your Hand*, Elizabeth Bennett
5	15	WL 4, 5	SL 7	TL 17, 18, 19, 20, 21	*What Happens to the Food We Eat?*; *Food From Around the World*

TERM 2

HALF-TERMLY PLANNER

Year 2 • Term 2 • Weeks 6–10

SCHOOL ____________________ **CLASS** ________ **TEACHER** ______________

		Phonetics, spelling and vocabulary	Grammar and punctuation	Comprehension and composition	Texts
Continuous work Weeks 6–10		WL 6, 7, 9, 12, 13 14	SL 1, 2, 3, 4, 9	TL 1, 2, 12	**Range** **Fiction and poetry:** traditional stories: stories and poems from other cultures; stories and poems with predictable and patterned language; poems by significant children's poets **Non-fiction:** (i) dictionaries, glossaries, indexes (ii) explanations
Blocked work					
Week	**Unit**				**Titles**
6	16	WL 1, 2, 4, 5	SL 7	TL 4, 5, 6, 7, 14	From *The Raja's Big Ears*, retold by Niru Desai
7	17	WL 3, 5, 11		TL 3, 4, 6, 7, 16	From *Why Snake Has No Legs*, retold by Ann Pilling
8	18	WL 2, 3	SL 7	TL 18, 19, 21	*Snake Charm*
9	19	WL 2, 8, 11		TL 3, 4, 5, 6, 13, 16, 17	From *Lao Lao of Dragon Mountain*, Margaret Bateson-Hill
10	20	WL 4, 5, 8	SL 7	TL 3, 5, 6, 14	From *Badger's Parting Gifts*, Susan Varley, Collins

Unit 11

A Kiss From a Princess

Key Learning Objectives

TL3	to discuss and compare story themes
TL4	to predict story endings/incidents, e.g. from unfinished extracts, while reading with the teacher
TL6	to identify and describe characters, expressing own views and using words and phrases from texts
TL7	to prepare and re-tell stories individually and through role-play in groups, using dialogue and narrative from text
WL3	to read and spell words containing the digraph *ph*
SL6	to identify speech marks in reading, understand their purpose and use the terms correctly

Range:	Fiction and poetry: traditional stories; stories with predictable and patterned language
Texts:	From *The Story of the Frog Prince,* retold by Margaret Carter From *The Princess and the Pig* in *The Triffic Pig Book,* Dick King-Smith
Resources:	Big Book 2B pp. 4–10 Pupil's Book 2 pp. 24–25 Copymasters 1, 10 and 11 Homework Book 2 p. 12

Preparation

- Day 2: you will need a trophy or a photograph to use as a prop.

DAY 1

Big Book 2B pp. 4–5; Pupil Book 2 pp. 24–25

Shared reading

- Find out how many children are familiar with the traditional story, "The Frog Prince". Ask them to tell you about the two main characters without giving away too much of the story.
- Read pages 4 and 5 together. What happened to the princess's golden ball? What did the frog want in return for fetching the princess's ball?
- Discuss the actions of the princess. What do the children think of the way she treated the frog?
- Can the children tell you what is going to happen next?

Focused word/sentence work

- Point out the traditional story opening, "Once upon a time. . ."
- Why is "PLOP!" printed in capital letters with an exclamation mark? How should it be read?
- Can the children explain what a "well" is? Perhaps they have read other versions of this story in which the well has been a lake or pond.
- What is a "companion"?

Independent work

- The questions on page 25 of Pupil Book 2 relate to today's extract from *The Story of the Frog Prince.*

Plenary

- How many other traditional stories can the children think of that contain a princess? Write the titles they offer you on the blackboard.
- Read through pages 4 and 5 again with the class.

DAY 2

Big Book 2B pp. 6–8; Pupil Book 2 p. 25

Shared reading

- Ask the children to remind you of the extract from *The Story of the Frog Prince* they read on Day 1.
- Read through pages 6 to 8 together. Talk about the ending. Can the children think of other traditional stories which end in this way, with the marriage of a prince and princess?

Focused word/sentence work

- Discuss the meaning of specific words and phrases, e.g. *motionless, hey presto.*
- Write the word *frog* on the board and underline the *f*. Challenge the class to think of another letter in the alphabet which makes the *f* sound. Write *p* on the board and explain that when *p* is followed by *h* the sound is *f* as in *frog*, not *p* as in *princess*. Give the children clues to words which contain the *ph* sound, e.g. *alphabet, dolphin, elephant, graph, photograph, telephone, trophy.* As they guess each word write it on the board and underline *ph*. Do not remove these words as they will be needed again in the plenary session.

Independent work

- The exercises for Days 2 and 3 on page 25 of Pupil Book 2 focus on the *ph* phoneme.

Plenary

- Hand a trophy or photograph to one of the children and ask him or her to read one of the words written on the board (during the focused word/sentence work) and then pass the prop to his or her neighbour. If a word was read correctly, rub it off the board.
- Once all the words have been read and rubbed off the board, the next child to receive the prop has to try and recall one of the words (or another word that contains *ph*) before passing it on. Write whatever word is given on the board. If it does not contain *ph* the children should tell you and you then rub it out.

DAY 3

Big Book 2B pp. 6–8; Pupil Book 2 p. 25

Shared reading

- Ask the class to retell the story of "The Frog Prince" from the point at which the princess runs away with her golden ball leaving the frog alone at the well.
- Read pages 6 to 8 again with the class. Discuss the differences between the children's combined oral account and the more formal written version.

Focused word/sentence work

- Focus on the use of speech marks in the story. Ask the children to find words spoken by the princess, her father and the frog. Read specific lines spoken by these characters together. Demonstrate how the speech marks mark out the words that are actually spoken by each character.

Independent work

- Complete exercises A and B on page 25 of Pupil Book 2 focusing on the *ph* phoneme.

Plenary

- Role-play some of the conversations between characters at different points in the story.
- Ask the children to look at home for different versions of this traditional story. Begin a class collection.

DAY 4

Pupil Book 2 pp. 24–25; Copymaster 10

Shared writing

- Read the first section of the extract from *The Story of the Frog Prince*, shown on page 24 of Pupil Book 2. Ask the children to tell you what happens next. Jot down the different stages as the children describe them.
- Read back the points that the class have outlined. Talk about how to develop these points into a story middle and ending.
- Use the children's suggestions to make the points into complete sentences.
- Encourage the children to contribute further details and descriptions to make their writing more interesting.

Focused word/sentence work

- Read together the shared writing that you have produced. Is there anything that the children would like to change?
- Identify any weak parts of the writing and refer back to the relevant part of the extract in Big Book 2B on pages 7 and 8 to compare and find a way to improve the weakness.
- Check the sentence punctuation together.

Independent work

- Give each child a copy of Copymaster 10 and ask them to continue the story of "The Frog Prince" in their own way, as described on page 25 of Pupil Book 2. Remind them that more time will be allowed to complete the story on Day 5.

Plenary

- Invite a few children to read their writing so far to the rest of the class. Encourage constructive criticism, noting the best features of each and suggesting ways to improve the writing.

DAY 5

Big Book 2B pp. 9–10; Copymaster 10 from Day 4

Shared reading

- Introduce the story of *The Princess and the Pig* by Dick King-Smith. Read page 9 with the class. Ask the children to predict how the story will end.
- Read page 10 with the class. Are the children surprised at the outcome of the story?
- Discuss the similarities and differences between this story and the traditional tale of "The Frog Prince".

Focused word/sentence work

- Focus on the speech marks. You may need to explain the way the words of the witch are set within the words spoken by the pig (who is reporting them).
- Try reading the spoken words together without the narration; divide the class in two with one half reading the part of the princess and the other half, the part of the pig.

Independent work

- The children should use this time to complete the writing they began on Day 4. Some children may, in the light of today's shared extract, like to consider writing a more original ending to their stories!

Plenary

- Invite different children to read their completed stories to the rest of the class. Draw attention to the best features of each child's writing.

Consolidation and extension

- Compare and contrast different versions of "The Frog Prince".
- Read other re-workings of traditional stories, with a piggy twist, from Dick King-Smith's *The Triffic Pig Book*.
- Use Copymaster 11 to create a passport for the princess.
- Use Copymaster 1 to practise spelling words containing *ph*.

Homework

- Page 12 in Homework Book 2 tests children's general knowledge of traditional stories.

Unit 12 All Pigs are Beautiful

Key Learning Objectives

TL16 to use dictionaries and glossaries to locate words by using initial letter

TL17 to learn that dictionaries and glossaries give definitions and explanations; discuss what definitions are, explore some simple definitions in dictionaries

TL18 to use other alphabetically ordered texts, e.g. indexes, directories, listings, registers; to discuss how they are used

WL10 to learn new words from reading linked to particular topics, to build individual collections of personal interest or significant words

WL11 to learn the use of antonyms and collect and discuss differences of meaning and their spelling

SL7 to investigate and recognise a range of other ways of presenting texts, e.g. speech bubbles, enlarged, bold or italicised print, captions, headings and sub-headings

Range:	Non fiction: alphabetically ordered texts
Texts:	From *All Pigs are Beautiful*, Dick King-Smith
Resources:	Big Book 2B pp. 11–15 Pupil Book 2 pp. 26–27 Copymaster 12 Homework Book 2 p. 13

Preparation

- Day 2: prepare two sets of word cards. Make the second set a different colour so that they may be easily distinguished from the first – set A: *up, hot, empty, happy, careful, loud*; set B: *down, cold, full, unhappy, careless, quiet.*
- Day 3: prepare a set of cards featuring the words of the index on page 15 of Big Book 2A: *bite, boar, food, gilts, mud, nests, piglets, sow.*
- Days 4 and 5: have available a range of appropriate dictionaries and, if possible, non-fiction books, for the children to refer to independently.

DAY 1

Big Book 2B pp. 11–13; Pupil Book 2 pp. 26–27

Shared reading

- Introduce the extract by Dick King-Smith. Read page 11 with the class. How many of the children would like to keep a pig as a pet? Discuss the problems that might arise from having such an unusual pet.
- Tell the children that Dick King-Smith was a farmer.
- Read pages 12 and 13.
- Read through the captions on pages 11 to 13. Explain their function.
- Compare this extract with *The Princess and the Pig* (also by Dick King-Smith) in the previous unit. Is this extract fiction or non-fiction? What is the difference?

Focused word/sentence work

- Can the children find a word on page 11 containing the spelling pattern *ou* as in *mouse* (*snouts*)? What is a snout? Can they find a word on page 13 that contains *ow* as in *clown* (*sows*)?
- Talk about Dick King-Smith's style of writing, which is less formal than many other examples of non-fiction.
- Look at some of the colloquialisms that Dick King-Smith uses, e.g. *soppy, grub* (page 12).

Independent work

- The questions on page 27 of Pupil Book 2 relate to today's extract from *All Pigs are Beautiful.*

Plenary

- See how much information the class can collectively recall. Close Big Book 2B and ask the children to tell you all the facts that they can remember. Jot down the facts on the board.
- Open Big Book 2B once more to verify the facts you have been given and see if there is any more information that the children did not recall.

DAY 2

Big Book 2B pp. 11–13; Pupil Book 2 p. 27

Shared reading

- Re-read pages 11 and 12.

Focused word/sentence work

- Write the first two sentences on page 11 on the board: "I love pigs. I don't care if they're little pigs or big pigs, with long snouts or short snouts, with ears that stick up or ears that flop down." Underline the words *little, long* and *up*. Ask the children to find a word that is opposite to each of the words that you have underlined (*big, short, down*). Underline each of these.
- Hand out the word cards (see **Preparation**) to different children. Choose someone from set A to read his or her card to the rest of the class. The child with the opposite word from set B should then read his or her card and join the first child.

Independent work

- The exercises on page 27 of Pupil Book 2 focus on antonyms.

Plenary

- Play the game of opposites (see **Focused word/sentence work** above) again with different children reading out the word cards.

DAY 3

Big Book 2B pp. 13–15; Pupil Book 2 p. 27

Shared reading

- Read pages 13 and 14 with the class.
- Re-read the last sentence on page 14. Does it sound familiar? Where have the children read it before (title)?
- Look at the index on page 15. Ask the children to select one of the words, e.g. *bite* and then turn back to the relevant page to find the reference to it. Repeat this with a few more words.
- Ask the children if they notice anything special about the way in which the words are listed. Can they explain why it is necessary to have indexes listed alphabetically? Do they know where to look for an index in a non-fiction book?

Focused word/sentence work

- Close Big Book 2B and hand out the word cards (see **Preparation**) to different children. Invite them out one at a time to stand at the front of the class. As each child comes to the front, he or she should read the word and stand in alphabetic sequence in the line, beginning with *bite* and ending with *sow*. It might be necessary to run through the alphabet a few times to assist children in finding the correct place to stand. Keep the word *boar* until last. Can any child suggest how to work out where it goes, given that *bite* also begins with *b*?
- Open Big Book 2B at page 15 to check the order that the children are standing in.

Independent work

- Use this time to complete the exercises on page 27 of Pupil Book 2.

Plenary

- Play the index word game (see **Focused word/sentence work** above) again with different children reading out the word cards.

DAY 4

Pupil Book 2 p. 27; Copymaster 12

Shared writing

- Read the writing task outlined on page 27 of Pupil Book 2. Check that the children fully understand the function of a glossary.
- Explain that you are going to practise making up a glossary about something else first. Choose a subject together and then ask the children to suggest associated words which it might be useful to include in a glossary. Write the suggestions in a column on the left hand side of the board. Discuss as a class which words to include and which to discount.

Focused word/sentence work

- Demonstrate how to use a dictionary to find the meaning of some of these words. For some of the words selected, the children may prefer to make up their own definitions. Discuss where else they might look to find the meaning of some of the words.
- Are the words listed alphabetically? If not, ask the class to help you put them into alphabetic order.

Independent work

- Using Copymaster 12, each child can attempt to produce his or her own "piggy" glossary. Make sure appropriate dictionaries (and non-fiction books if possible) are available for reference. The children might find it useful to work in pairs for this activity.

Plenary

- Discuss the children's progress with their pig glossaries. Are there any other "piggy" words which they would like to include? Write down any suggestions so that the children who wish to may add them to their glossaries on Day 5.

DAY 5

Big Book 2B pp. 13–15; Pupil Book 2 p. 27; Copymaster 12 from Day 4

Shared reading

- Re-read pages 13 and 14. Can the children recall from these pages, and the others they have read on previous days, all the things that Dick King-Smith says he likes most about pigs?

Focused word/sentence work

- Focus on the index on page 15 once more. Take each word in turn and ask the children to remind you of the information that Dick King-Smith gave relating to each, e.g. *bite* ("you be careful – pigs have a horrible bite"). If the children are unable to recall the information that was given about a particular word, look up the page reference in order to locate it.

Independent work

- Allow time for the children to finish their glossaries and write a few sentences using some of the words listed. Children who complete this task within the given time may like to look for glossaries in a range of non-fiction books.

Plenary

- Ask the children who were looking for glossaries in non-fiction books to show the class examples. Note that these, like indexes, are usually found in the back of non-fiction books.

Consolidation and extension

- Read *All Pigs are Beautiful* by Dick King-Smith in its entirety. Compare it with other non-fiction books about pigs.
- Ask the children to make their own information books, with indexes, about their favourite animals or pets.

Homework

- Page 13 in Homework Book 2 consolidates work on indexes.

Unit 13

Dog, Cat and Monkey

Key Learning Objectives

TL4	to predict story endings/incidents, e.g. from unfinished extracts, while reading with the teacher
TL6	to identify and describe characters, expressing own views and using words and phrases from texts
TL7	to prepare and re-tell stories individually and through role-play in groups, using dialogue and narrative from text
WL2	to learn the common spelling patterns for the vowel phonemes *air*, *or* and *er*
SL5	to use verb tenses with increasing accuracy in speaking and writing, and to use past tense consistently for narration

Range:	Fiction and poetry: stories from other cultures
Texts:	From *Dog, Cat and Monkey* in *The Oxfam Book of Children's Stories,* ed. Michael Rosen
Resources:	Big Book 2B pp. 16–20 Pupil Book 2 pp. 28–29 Copymasters 1, 11 and 13 Homework Book 2 p. 14

Preparation

- Day 1: you will need a globe or map of the world.

DAY 1

Big Book 2B pp. 16–17; Pupil Book 2 pp. 28–29

Shared reading

- Introduce the story extract *Dog, Cat and Monkey* which comes from Indonesia. Find Indonesia on a globe or map of the world and show where it is in relation to Britain.
- Read page 16 together. Why are Dog and Cat fighting? What do the children think of Monkey's advice?
- Read page 17. What is Monkey going to use the scales for? Do the children think he will be able to sort out the disagreement? Encourage them to speculate on the outcome of this story.

Focused word/sentence work

- Write Monkey's advice on the board: "Go on, Cat, go for it with the claws, now the teeth. You've got him now, Dog. Grind those jaws." Read the sentences with the class. Underline *aw* in the words *claws* and *jaws*. Ask the children to say the vowel phoneme you have underlined.
- Generate a rhyming string of words ending in the spelling pattern *aw*, e.g. *claw, draw, jaw, law, paw, straw.*

Independent work

- Children answer the comprehension questions on page 29 of Pupil Book 2.

Plenary

- Re-read pages 16 and 17.

DAY 2

Big Book 2B pp. 18–19; Pupil Book 2 p. 29

Shared reading

- Ask the class to retell the beginning of the story of *Dog, Cat and Monkey*.
- Read pages 18 and 19. Discuss Monkey's actions; is he acting in the interests of the other animals? Can the children predict what the outcome of this story will be?

Focused word/sentence work

- Discuss the way the story is written, in the present tense rather than the past. You may like to refer back to other stories to show how they are usually written in the past tense and contrast them with this one. Can the children find words in the text which suggest the story is happening now, e.g. "Dog and Cat *are* fighting over some meat" (rather than "Dog and Cat *were* fighting over some meat")?

Independent work

- The exercises on page 29 of Pupil Book 2 focus on past and present tense verbs.

Plenary

- Give sentences in the present tense and ask the children to give the same sentences in the past tense, e.g. "Ania *is throwing* the ball to Aislinn"; "Ania *threw* the ball to Aislinn". You may like to incorporate mime into your sentences to reinforce the "action" words in each.

DAY 3

Big Book 2B pp. 18–20; Pupil Book 2 p. 29

Shared reading

- Re-read page 18 before moving on to read the conclusion to *Dog, Cat and Monkey* on pages 19 and 20.
- Discuss whether or not the story ended in the way that the children predicted it would. Is there a lesson to be learned from this story?

Focused word/sentence work

- Write the following words from page 18 on the board: *proper, lower, heavier* and *cleverness*. Underline *er* in each word. Read the words together and listen to the phoneme you have underlined.

- Focus particularly on the word *lower*. Explain how *-er* is often added to the end of a word to mean "more of" something. Demonstrate this by asking two of the tallest children to stand. Say *"Anusha" is tall but "Michael" is taller*. Write your sentence on the board. Give other examples of comparitive adjectives. Refer back to the word *heavier* on page 18. Explain how this is another example of a word with an *-er* ending to show "more of"; one piece of meat was *more heavy* (*heavier*) than the other. Point out that when adding *-er* to a word that ends in *y*, the *y* changes to an *i*.

Independent work

- Complete the exercises on page 29 of Pupil Book 2.

Plenary

- Re-enact the story of *Dog, Cat and Monkey* through role-play, using dialogue from the text.

DAY 4

Big Book 2B pp. 18–19; Pupil Book 2 p. 29; Copymaster 13

Shared writing

- Introduce the writing task outlined on page 29 of Pupil Book 2. Think about the story from Monkey's perspective. What is Monkey's opinion of Dog and Cat?
- Write a first draft of the story from Monkey's perspective together. Emphasise the fact that the story is being reported by Monkey in the past tense. Refer to the story extract in Big Book 2B if the children need reminding of the plot.

Focused word/sentence work

- Read through the first draft together. Check the organisation of the events in the story. Check for consistency of tense. Can the children find ways to improve their writing?
- Check the sentence punctuation together.

Independent work

- Ask the children to begin writing their own retelling of the story, using Copymaster 13.

Plenary

- Invite a few of the children to read their writing so far. Encourage the rest of the class to identify the best features of each.

DAY 5

Big Book 2B pp. 18–20; Pupil Book 2 p. 29; Copymaster 13 from Day 4

Shared reading

- Re-read pages 18–20. Discuss how Dog and Cat could have had half of the meat each if they had shared the meat, whereas they ended up with nothing.

Focused word/sentence work

- Write the word *share* on the board. Read the word together. Underline *are* and ask the children to say aloud the vowel phoneme. Generate a rhyming string of words ending in the spelling pattern *are*, e.g. *care, dare, fare, hare, rare, stare*. The children will probably suggest words ending in *ear*, e.g. *bear*; *air*, e.g. *fair*; or *-ere*, e.g. *there*. Write these words in separate lists. Discuss the different meanings of any homophones that emerge from the lists, e.g. *bare/bear*; *fare/fair*; *hare/hair*.

Independent work

- Children complete the writing they began on Day 4.

Plenary

- Invite different children to read their completed stories.

Consolidation and extension

- Use Copymaster 1 to practise spelling words containing *are* as in *share*.
- Use Copymaster 11 to create a passport for Monkey.

Homework

- Page 14 in Homework Book 2 focuses on the spelling patterns for the vowel phoneme *er*.

Unit 14 Food From Far and Wide

Key Learning Objectives

TL8	to read own poems aloud
TL9	to identify and discuss patterns of rhythm, rhyme and other features of sound in different poems
TL10	to comment on and recognise when the reading aloud of a poem makes sense and is effective
TL11	to identify and discuss favourite poems and poets, using appropriate terms (*poet, poem, verse, rhyme*, etc.) and referring to the language of the poems
TL15	to use structures from poems as a basis for writing, by extending or substituting elements, inventing own lines, verses; to make class collections, illustrated with captions; to write own poems from initial jottings and words
WL2	to learn the common spelling patterns for the vowel phoneme *or*
WL10	to learn new words from reading linked to particular topics, to build individual collections of personal interest or significant words
SL8	to use commas to separate items in a list

Range:	Poetry: poems with predictable and patterned language
Texts:	*Chips*, Stanley Cook *Spaghetti! Spaghetti!*, Jack Prelutsky *Hot Food*, Michael Rosen *Chapatti in Your Hand*, Elizabeth Bennett
Resources:	Big Book 2B pp. 21–26 Pupil Book 2 pp. 30–31 Copymaster 14 Homework Book 2 p. 15

DAY 1

Big Book 2B pp. 21–23; Pupil Book 2 pp. 30–31

Shared reading

- Read the poem *Chips* by Stanley Cook, on page 21 of Big Book 2B. How many children have eaten chips from a paper bag? Look at the contrast between the first and last verses (focus on the references to hot and cold). Note how the poem ends with the line, "But the chips and I are warm inside". What do the children think about this ending?
- Read *Spaghetti! Spaghetti!* by Jack Prelutsky, on pages 22 and 23. Ask the children to tell you about the difficulties they have encountered when trying to eat spaghetti. Encourage them to describe the taste, texture and smell of spaghetti. What do they like best about this poem?

Focused word/sentence work

- Look again at *Chips* by Stanley Cook. Ask the children to find the rhyming pair in each verse (*chips/lips; shakes/snowflakes; slide/inside*). Discuss the way the poet describes the salt and vinegar which are shaken over the hot chips:

  "Raindrops of vinegar . . .
  And salty snowflakes".

  Point out the alliteration in *salty snowflakes*. Can the children find two more words close together which begin with the same letters in the third verse ("slippery as a slide")?
- Look at *Spaghetti! Spaghetti!* by Jack Prelutsky. Can the children find the rhyming pairs in each verse (*stuff/enough; cheese/please; mound/around; plate/great; lot/hot*)? Have they noticed the repetition? Can they tell you how many lines there are in each verse? Point out the alliteration.

Independent work

- The questions on page 31 of Pupil Book 2 relate to the poems by Stanley Cook and Jack Prelutsky.

Plenary

- Re-read the two poems with the class. Ask the children to tell you which of the two poems they prefer, giving reasons for their preferences. Encourage them to use the terms "poem", "verse", "rhyme" and "poet".

DAY 2

Big Book 2B pp. 24–25; Pupil Book 2 pp. 30–31

Shared reading

- Introduce the poem *Hot Food* by Michael Rosen. Do any of the children remember reading any other poems of stories by Michael Rosen? (*Dog, Cat and Monkey*, Unit 13) Read through the poem.
- Can the children recall putting something in their mouths which was too hot for them? Did they react in the same way as Dad?
- Read the poem a second time with the class.

Focused word/sentence work

- Talk about the style of this poem. Can the children find words and phrases which are repeated? Which word has Michael Rosen used to describe the sound of blowing on the hot food to cool it down? What do the children like best about the poem?
- In preparation for today's independent work, demonstrate how commas are used within lists. Ask a few children to tell you what their favourite foods are and write these within a sentence, e.g. *Our favourite foods are chocolate, chips, bananas and sausages.*
- Show how we use commas when there are more than two items. Point out that a comma is not necessary immediately before the word *and*.
- Write a few more lists like this and invite children to show you where the commas should go.

Independent work

- The exercises for Days 2 and 3 on page 31 of Pupil Book 2 provide practice in using commas in lists.

Plenary

- Read the poem *Hot Food* by Michael Rosen again with the class. Introduce a few actions.

DAY 3

Big Book 2B p. 26; Pupil Book 2 p. 31

Shared reading

- Read the final poem in this unit, *Chapatti in Your Hand* by Elizabeth Bennett. Talk about the different foods mentioned in the rhyme. How many children have tried chapattis, or prawn balls? Do they know which countries these foods come from? How many children have seen a chapatti being made or tried using chopsticks?
- Re-read the poem together. You may like to introduce a few simple actions.

Focused word/sentence work

- Look at the structure of the poem. Which lines are repeated?
- Write the word *prawn* on the board and underline *aw*. Give clues to other words which contain the *aw* phoneme, e.g. a tool with sharp teeth used to cut wood (*saw*); you do this when you are tired (*yawn*). As each word is correctly guessed, write it on the board and underline *aw*.
- Write the word *fork* on the board and underline *or*. Compare the sound of *or* with *aw* in *prawn*. Give clues to other words which contain *or*, e.g. *corner, forgive, important, order, platform, report, short, sort, storm, story, torch*. Again, as each word is correctly guessed, write it on the board and underline *or*.

Independent work

- Children complete the exercises on page 31 of Pupil Book 2.

Plenary

- Try extemporising on the pattern established in Elizabeth Bennett's poem. In *This Little Puffin*, Elizabeth Bennett suggests using the following ideas, or any others the children think of, which can be fitted to the rhythm: soup in a bowl, sandwich in your fingers, sausages on sticks, etc.

DAY 4

Pupil Book 2 p. 31

Shared writing

- Introduce the independent writing task outlined on page 31 of Pupil Book 2. Decide on a type of food and focus on this together before attempting to put all the ideas together in a poem.
- Ask the children to contribute words to describe the taste, smell, look and feel of your chosen food. Talk about different ways of serving the favourite food. Build up a wordbank of adjectives and ideas.
- Help the children to draw the best ideas and most effective vocabulary from the wordbank and create a poem.

Focused word/sentence work

- Emphasize that a poem is simply the best words in the best order. Dissuade the children from focusing on rhyme (other than rhyming pairs which they may want to draw from the poems they have read) as this distracts them from finding the most effective vocabulary. You may like to loosely adopt the format of one of the poems you have shared this week, e.g.

  I love sausages,
  I can't get enough.
  Sausages! Sausages!
  So wonderful to eat!
  Sausage rolls and sausages on sticks,
  Sausage with mustard and sausages with chips.
  You sizzle and frazzle in the frying pan
  And fill the air with fried sausage scent.

Independent work

- The children could use this time to experiment with their own ideas for a poem about their favourite foods.

Plenary

- Listen to a few of the children's ideas. Discuss ways of improving them and encourage the class to tell you what they like best about each poem so far.

DAY 5

Big Book 2B pp. 21–26; Copymaster 14

Shared reading

- Survey the class on their favourite of the week's four poems. Re-read the children's favourites together, asking them to explain what it is about the poems that appeals to them most of all.

Focused word/sentence work

- Reinforce the terms *poem, poet, verse* and *rhyme* in your discussion with the children.

Independent work

- The children could use this time to improve their own poetry writing. The completed poems could be presented in best handwriting on Copymaster 14.

Plenary

- Choose different children to read aloud their completed poems and show how they have presented them.

Consolidation and extension

- Begin a collection of poetry about food. Ask each child to choose his or her favourite, write it out in best handwriting and illustrate it for a class anthology.
- Look at a variety of menus.

Homework

- Page 15 in Homework Book 2 requires the children to write a menu of their own choosing.

Unit 15 The Food We Eat

Key Learning Objectives

TL17	to learn that dictionaries and glossaries give definitions and explanations
TL18	to use other alphabetically ordered texts, e.g. indexes, directories, listings, registers; to discuss how they are used
TL19	to read flow charts and cyclical diagrams that explain a process
TL20	to make class dictionaries and glossaries of special interest words, giving explanations and definitions
TL21	to produce simple flow charts or diagrams that explain a process
WL4	to split familiar oral and written compound words into their component parts
WL5	to discriminate, orally, syllables in multi-syllabic words using children's names and words from their reading. Extend to written forms and note syllable boundary in speech and writing
SL7	to investigate and recognise a range of other ways of presenting texts

Range:	Non-fiction: indexes and other alphabetically ordered texts; explanations
Texts:	*What Happens to the Food We Eat?* *Food From Around the World*
Resources:	Big Book 2B pp. 27–30 Pupil Book 2 pp. 32–33 Copymaster 15 Homework Book 2 p. 16

Preparation

- Day 2: you will need a globe or map of the world.
- Day 3: the children will need access to a variety of appropriate non-fiction books with indexes.
- Day 4: you will need a length of string (equal to the width of the classroom) to make a "washing line", pegs or paperclips and a set of cards with food names on them, e.g. *apple, banana, crisps, potato, rice.*

DAY 1

Big Book 2B pp. 27–28; Pupil Book 2 pp. 32–33

Shared reading

- What is the main heading of this unit? What is the sub-heading on page 27? Read page 27 with the class. Can the children tell you whether the text is fiction or non-fiction?
- Read page 28. Discuss the process of digestion in simple terms.

Focused word/sentence work

- Explain the unfamiliar terms: *chemicals, digestion, intestines.* Break the words down into syllables orally, to help the children pronounce them.
- Note the soft *g* sound in the words *energy* and *digest.*
- Listen to the sound of *ch* in *chemicals.* Write other examples on the board for the class to read, e.g. *echo, Christmas, Christopher, school.*
- Break the information on page 28 down into stages. Write these on the board and number them, *1) You swallow food; 2) It travels down a tube into your tummy;* etc.

Independent work

- The questions on page 33 of Pupil Book 2 relate to today's non-fiction text.

Plenary

- Talk about the way the information on page 32 of Pupil Book 2 is presented. Compare this with the text on page 28 of Big Book 2B. Discuss which of the two texts presents the information most clearly.

DAY 2

Big Book 2B pp. 29–30; Pupil Book 2 p. 33

Shared reading

- Can the class read the sub-heading on page 29? Read together pages 29 and 30. Ask literal questions about the text: Why are some of the foods we eat bought from other countries? Name two countries where rice is grown. Name some fruits that grow easily in Britain. Name some foods which are grown in hotter countries. Name two countries where tea is grown.
- Find China and India on a globe or map of the world. Think about the distance of each of these countries from Britain. Have any of the children travelled to either of these countries? Can they remember how long the journey was?
- How many of the children's families grow fruit and vegetables to eat?

Focused word/sentence work

- Can the children explain the meaning of the word "abroad"?
- Write the word *supermarket* on the board. Can the children see two smaller words within this word? How many syllables can they hear when they say the word aloud?
- Write the word *sunshine* on the board. Again, can the children see two smaller words within this word? How many syllables can they hear?
- How many syllables are there in the words *rice* and *potatoes*?
- Read through the index on page 33 of Pupil Book 2 together. Discuss any unfamiliar vocabulary.

Independent work

- There are questions on page 33 of Pupil Book 2 relating to the index you have read together.

Plenary

- Write a list of foods from page 30 on the board (*apples, pears, berries, oranges, lemons, pineapples, coffee, tea, sugar, bananas*). Read the words one at a time together and ask the children to tell you how many syllables there are in each.

DAY 3

Big Book 2B pp. 27–28; Pupil Book 2 p. 33

Shared reading

- Re-read pages 27 and 28 together.

Focused word/sentence work

- Look again at the index on page 33 of Pupil Book 2. Revise the unfamiliar terms.

Independent work

- When the children have completed the exercises on page 33 of Pupil Book 2, give them time to practise using an index with a partner.

Plenary

- Ask a few of the children to share with the class the non-fiction books they have been looking at. Ask them to tell you what it was that they wanted to look up. Were they able to find it using the index? Can they remember what the book said about it?

DAY 4

Pupil Book 2 p. 33; Copymaster 15

Shared writing

- Read through the writing task outlined on page 33 of Pupil Book 2. Ask the children to tell you some of their favourite foods. Write six of them on the board. Ask the children to help you list the six foods in alphabetical order.
- Ask the children to think of a brief description for each food. You might like to begin with dictionary definitions.

Focused word/sentence work

- Using a low "washing line" made of string, hand a group of children the word cards you have prepared and ask them to attach the words to the line in alphabetic order. As each child takes his or her turn, the rest of the class should assist in deciding which words need to be moved along to make room for the new word.

Independent work

- Using Copymaster 15, the children can each choose their six favourite foods and list them in alphabetic order with descriptions.

Plenary

- Invite a few children to show their food charts to the class. The others should check that the foods have been listed in alphabetic order.

DAY 5

Big Book 2B pp. 29–30; Pupil Book 2 p. 32; Copymaster 15 from Day 4

Shared reading

- Re-read page 32 of Pupil Book 2 together, showing a flow chart diagram of the process of digestion. Talk about the way the information is presented.

Focused word/sentence work

- Ask the children to help you construct a flow chart diagram to show "the journey of tea", drawing on the information they have read on pages 29 and 30 of Big Book 2B (you may need to refer back to these pages).
  1. Tea leaves grow in India or China.
  2. The tea is picked.
  3. The tea is transported to Britain (can the children tell you how?).
  4. The tea is packed and sent to shops around Britain.
  5. We buy the tea from the supermarket and take it to our homes.

Independent work

- The children should complete their food charts using Copymaster 15, and illustrate their chosen foods.

Plenary

- Choose different children to show their completed food charts to the class. Again, the others should check that the foods have been listed in alphabetic order. Which of the descriptions do they think are the most effective?

Consolidation and extension

- The children's food charts could be compiled to make a class dictionary of food, or used to make a database of favourite foods.
- Make a collection of food labels. Display these around a map of the world, indicating where each product has come from.

Homework

- Page 16 in Homework Book 2 presents a flow diagram to show how a cup of tea is made.

Unit 16 The Raja's Big Ears

Key Learning Objectives

TL4	to predict story endings/incidents, e.g. from unfinished extracts, while reading with the teacher
TL5	to discuss story settings: to compare differences; to locate key words and phrases in text; to consider how different settings influence events and behaviour
TL6	to identify and describe characters, expressing own views and using words and phrases from texts
TL7	to prepare and re-tell stories individually and through role-play in groups, using dialogue and narrative from text
TL14	to write character profiles, e.g. simple descriptions, posters, passports, using key words and phrases that describe or are spoken by characters in the text
WL1	to secure the reading and spelling of words containing different spellings of the long vowel phonemes from Year 1
WL2	to learn the common spelling patterns for the vowel phoneme *air*
WL4	to split familiar oral and written compound words into their component parts
WL5	to discriminate, orally, syllables in multi-syllabic words using children's names and words from their reading. Extend to written forms and note syllable boundary in speech and writing
SL7	to investigate and recognise a range of other ways of presenting texts, e.g. speech bubbles, enlarged, bold or italicised print, captions, headings and sub-heading

Range:	Fiction: stories from other cultures
Texts:	From *The Raja's Big Ears*, retold by Niru Desai
Resources:	Big Book 2B pp. 31–38 Pupil Book 2 pp. 34–35 Copymasters 1, 11 and 16 Homework Book 2 p. 17

Preparation

- Day 2: you will need a drum that can be passed around the class.

DAY 1

Big Book 2B pp. 31–33; Pupil Book 2 pp. 34–35

Shared reading

- Introduce the story of *The Raja's Big Ears* by Niru Desai. Read through the first three pages of the extract with the children. Explain the meaning of the words *Raja* (an Indian prince or king) and *topee* (a headdress).
- Do the children know what a barber is? How does Manji know the Raja's secret?
- Discuss whether the Raja is likely to find out that Manji has told his secret to a tree. What do the children think people would say if they discovered that their Raja has big ears?

Focused word/sentence work

- Look at the story opening, "Once upon a time. . . " Do the children recognise this as a traditional way of starting a story? How do stories that begin in this way usually end?
- Write the word *topee* on the board and underline *ee*. Ask the children to say aloud the sound you have underlined.
- Write the following sentences on the board: "The leaves on the tree rustled in the breeze." "He knew that trees cannot speak." Ask five volunteers to each come and underline one *ee/ea* sound. Give clues to words other than *topee* which end in *-ee*, e.g. *coffee, free, knee, see, tree*. The children may suggest other words which end with the same phoneme but a different spelling pattern, e.g. *-ey* (as in *key, money, monkey*) or *-ea* (as in *flea, pea, tea*).

Independent work

- The questions on page 35 of Pupil Book 2 relate to today's extract from *The Raja's Big Ears*.

Plenary

- Re-read pages 31 to 33.

DAY 2

Big Book 2B pp. 34–35; Pupil Book 2 p. 35

Shared reading

- Ask the class to remind you of the story so far.
- Read page 34. Explain that a *tabla* is a percussion instrument consisting of two drums played with the hands. Can the children tell you what a musician is?
- Read page 35 together. Ask the children to suggest what might happen next.

Focused word/sentence work

- Write the word *elephant* on the board. Draw the children's attention to the *ph* sound. How many syllables can the children hear?
- Write the words *woodcutter, craftsmen, birthday* and *everyone* on the board. Can the children identify two smaller words within each word?

Independent work

- Page 35 of Pupil Book 2 focuses on the common spelling patterns for the vowel phoneme *air*.

Plenary

- Pass a drum around the class. As each child takes the drum, he or she says his or her own name and beats the drum once for each syllable simultaneously. For example, Nicola would beat the drum three times: *Ni/co/la*.
- The children could get into groups according to the number of syllables in their names.

DAY 3

Big Book 2B pp. 36–38; Pupil Book 2 p. 35

Shared reading

- Recap on the story of *The Raja's Big Ears* with the children. Read the conclusion to the story on pages 36 to 38.
- Discuss the story's ending. Did the children expect it to be resolved in this way? Do they like the way the story ended or did they have better ideas of their own?

Focused word/sentence work

- Discuss the way Manji's stutter is presented in the text on page 36.
- Look at the way ellipses are used to denote a pause.
- Can the children find another title used by Manji for the Raja, on page 36 (*Your Highness*)? Can they find two words on page 38 which describe the Raja (*kind* and *fair*)?

Independent work

- The second exercise for Days 2 and 3 on page 35 of Pupil Book 2 requires children to contextualise words with different spelling patterns of the vowel phoneme *air*, within sentences of their own.

Plenary

- Re-tell the final scene of *The Raja's Big Ears* together through role-play.

DAY 4

Big Book 2B pp 32–38; Pupil Book 2 p. 35; Copymaster 16

Shared writing

- Read the writing task outlined on page 35 of Pupil Book 2 with the class. Focus on the Raja for this session. With the children's help, scan this week's story again for references to the Raja and write the information about him on the board. Agree with the children a key phrase or sentence spoken by the Raja and write this down too.
- Organise your writing into different sections covering the following: What does the Raja look like? What is his role? How would you describe his character?

Focused word/sentence work

- Review the shared writing together looking for opportunities to improve it. Have the children selected the best possible adjectives to describe the Raja? Have they used key words and phrases from the text?
- Check the sentence punctuation together.

Independent work

- Using Copymaster 16, the children may write their own character profile of the Raja. There is a speech bubble next to the illustration of the Raja for the children to write a memorable line spoken by the Raja in the story. Explain that the children should not begin their description of Manji until Day 5.

Plenary

- Invite some of the children to read out their character profiles. Decide as a class whether each description is an accurate one. Find out which line spoken by the Raja has been used most by the class.

DAY 5

Big Book 2B pp. 32–38; Pupil Book 2 p. 35; Copymaster 16 from Day 4

Shared reading/writing

- Turn your attention to Manji for this session. Scan the story again for references to Manji and collate the information about him on the board. Agree with the children a key phrase or sentence spoken by him and write this down too.
- Organise your writing into different sections covering the following: What does Manji look like? What is his job? How would you describe his character?

Focused word/sentence work

- As before, review the shared writing together looking for opportunities to improve it. Have the children selected the best possible adjectives to describe Manji? Have they used key words and phrases from the text?
- Check the sentence punctuation together.

Independent work

- Once the children have completed their character profiles of the Raja, using Copymaster 16, they may begin writing a description of Manji. There is another speech bubble next to the illustration of Manji for the children to write a memorable line spoken by him in the story.

Plenary

- Invite different children to read out their completed character profiles. Have they referred to all of the areas that you focused on together (appearance, occupation and personality)?

Consolidation and extension

- Copymaster 11 could be used for the children to complete a "passport" for either the Raja or Manji.
- Read the story of *The Raja's Big Ears* in its entirety. The book is a dual language book (told also in Punjabi).
- Use Copymaster 1 to practise spelling words containing the vowel phoneme *air*.

Homework

- Page 17 of Homework Book 2 focuses on the common spelling patterns for the vowel phoneme *air*.

Unit 17

Why Snake Has No Legs

Key Learning Objectives

TL3	to discuss and compare story themes
TL4	to predict story endings/incidents, e.g. from unfinished extracts, while reading with the teacher
TL6	to identify and describe characters, expressing own views and using words and phrases from texts
TL7	to prepare and re-tell stories individually and through role-play in groups, using dialogue and narrative from text
TL16	to use dictionaries to locate words by using initial letter
WL3	to read and spell words containing the digraphs *wh* and *ch* (as in *Christopher*)
WL5	to discriminate, orally, syllables in multi-syllabic words using children's names and words from their reading. Extend to written forms and note syllable boundary in speech and writing
WL11	to learn the use of antonyms and collect and discuss differences of meaning and their spelling.

Range:	Fiction: stories from other cultures
Texts:	From *Why Snake Has No Legs*, retold by Ann Pilling
Resources:	Big Book 2B pp. 39–45 Pupil Book 2 pp. 36–37 Copymasters 1 and 17 Homework Book 2 p. 18

Preparation

- Day 3: the children will need dictionaries for independent work.

DAY 1

Big Book 2B pp. 39–41; Pupil Book 2 pp. 36–37

Shared reading

- Introduce the story *Why Snake Has No Legs*, an Ashanti story from Ghana. Read pages 39–40. Ask the children to describe the character of Snake. What do the other animals think of him?
- Read page 41 together. Who was the wisest creature of all? What was Ananse's plan? Can the children explain how it will work? Can they guess who the thief might be?

Focused word/sentence work

- Can the children find words on page 39 that mean *cosy* (*snug*) and *lazy* (*idle*)?
- Look at page 40. Can the children find words that mean the opposite of *good* (*bad*), *old* (*new*), *down* (*up*), *right* (*wrong*), *noisy* (*quiet*), *easy* (*hard*)?
- Explain the meaning of *harvest*.

Independent work

- The questions on page 37 of Pupil Book 2 will test children's comprehension of today's extract.

Plenary

- Retell the beginning of the story through role-play. On this occasion work with a group of volunteers to begin with. One child, playing the part of Snake, should give excuses as to why he cannot help the other animals. Draw other children into the drama by asking them what they think about Snake's idle behaviour.

DAY 2

Big Book 2B pp. 41–43; Pupil Book 2 p. 37

Shared reading

- Re-read page 41 with the class.
- Now read pages 42 and 43. Are the children surprised by the revelation that it was Snake who was stealing the crops? How do the children think the story will end? Will the other animals forgive Snake?

Focused word/sentence work

- Point to the phrase "clever spider" on page 42. Can the children identify the sound that is the same in both words (*er*)? Challenge them to think of months of the year that end in *-er*, e.g. *September, October, November, December* or family names, e.g. *sister, brother, mother, father*.
- Can the children explain the phrase, "the other animals showed him no mercy" on page 43?
- Can they find the words that the other animals shout at Snake (*Thief!; Lazy thief!*)? Identify the speech marks enclosing the spoken words. Discuss the function of the exclamation marks.

Independent work

- Exercise A on page 37 of Pupil Book 2 poses further questions based on this week's story extract. The children's attention is then drawn to the words which begin the questions and the initial digraph *wh-*.

Plenary

- Write the questioning words *why, when, who, where, which, what* on the board. Ask the children to think of questions beginning with these words to ask the rest of the class.
- Extend this activity by providing answers and asking the children to think about what question might have been asked to lead to your answer, e.g. *I live in Liverpool.* (*Where do you live?*) *Today is Tuesday.* (*What day is it?*)
- Can the children think of any other questioning words that begin with another letter, e.g. *how?*

DAY 3

Big Book 2B pp. 43–45; Pupil Book 2 p. 37

Shared reading

- Re-read page 43 before reading the conclusion on pages 44 and 45. What do the children think about the way the story ends? Do they feel sorry for Snake?

Focused word/sentence work

- Look at the word *unstick* on page 43. Explain that the prefix *un-* changes the meaning of a word. Write some examples on the board, e.g. *unfinished, unhappy, unlucky.* Are the children able to tell you how the prefix *un-* changes a word?
- Listen to the sound of *u* in the word *pull.* Why is the word "PULLED", on page 44, printed in capital letters?
- Look at page 44. Discuss the effectiveness of the onomatopoeic words, *Gloopity-gloop* and *whooshing.* Point out the *wh* digraph in *whooshing.*

Independent work

- When the children have completed exercises A and B on page 37 of Pupil Book 2, challenge them to find more words beginning with *wh* in a dictionary. Ask them to write down the words they find, perhaps illustrating one or two of them.

Plenary

- Ask the children who used dictionaries to find words beginning with *wh* to report back to the class the words that they find. Can the class tell you how many syllables there are in some of these words? Challenge them to put some of the words into sentences orally.

DAY 4

Pupil Book 2 pp. 36–37

Shared writing

- Introduce the writing task set out on page 37 of Pupil Book 2. Decide on a theme for your story, e.g. why the giraffe has such a long neck, and write a title on the board. Ask the class to think of as many different reasons as they can, explaining the title. For example: *When the world was still very new the giraffe looked more like a horse. He was a very nosy character, always poking his nose into everyone's business. One day he poked his nose down a rabbit warren and ended up getting his head stuck. As a result of the animals trying to pull him free, his neck was stretched. Fortunately, the giraffe was quite pleased with his new, longer neck as it meant he could reach the leaves right at the tops of the trees.*
- Once you have established a plan for your class story, help the children to develop their ideas and put them into complete sentences.

Focused word/sentence work

- Review the shared writing together looking for opportunities to improve it. Perhaps the children could be encouraged to improve their choice of vocabulary and add one or two descriptive phrases to enhance their writing.
- Check the sentence punctuation together.

Independent work

- The children could now begin writing their own stories, using the idea developed during your shared writing session, or others of their own. Suggest that they use the story opener on page 36 of Pupil Book 2: "When the world was still very new. . ."

Plenary

- Invite a few of the children to read aloud their story beginnings. As always, use this opportunity to draw the rest of the children's attention to the best features of each. Encourage them to think of suggestions for each child on how to develop their stories.

DAY 5

Big Book 2B pp. 43–45

Shared reading

- Re-read pages 43 to 45. Discuss the way the story is concluded and relate your discussion to the story ending you decided upon on Day 4 for your shared writing. Do the children think that the explanation for Snake's lack of legs is a good one?

Focused word/sentence work

- Can the children find words on pages 44 and 45 that mean the opposite of *forwards* (*backwards*), *bottom* (*top*), *right* (*wrong*), *same* (*different*), *fat* (*thin*)?
- Point out the digraph *ch* in "stomach". What sound does it make in this word? What sound does it usually make? Give clues to other words containing this digraph and sound as in *stomach*, e.g. *school, choir, Christmas, echo.*

Independent work

- The children should use this time to finish their stories. Children who complete their stories within the twenty minutes may like to illustrate them with a "Before" and "After" picture of their animal character.

Plenary

- Choose different children to read aloud their completed stories. Invite the rest of the class to tell the children what they like best about their stories.

Consolidation and extension

- Copymaster 17 focuses on the digraph *ch* as in *school.*
- Use Copymaster 1 to practise the spellings of other words beginning with *wh.*

Homework

- Page 18 of Homework Book 2 provides dictionary skills practice, focusing on words beginning with *wh.*

Unit 18 Snake Charm

Key Learning Objectives

TL18 to use other alphabetically ordered texts, e.g. indexes; to discuss how they are used

TL19 to read flow charts and cyclical diagrams that explain a process

TL21 to produce simple flow charts or diagrams that explain a process

WL2 to learn the common spelling patterns for the vowel phonemes *or* and *er*

WL3 to read and spell words containing the digraph *wh*

SL7 to investigate and recognise a range of other ways of presenting texts, e.g. speech bubbles, enlarged, bold or italicised print, captions, headings and sub-headings

Range:	Non-fiction: dictionaries, glossaries, indexes and other alphabetically ordered texts; explanations
Texts:	*Snake Charm*
Resources:	Big Book 2B pp. 46–50 Pupil Book 2 pp. 38–39 Copymasters 1 and 18 Homework Book 2 p.19

Preparation

- Days 3 and 4: make a selection of word cards with words containing *er*, *ir* and *ur*, e.g. *after, brother, flower, her, monster, other, over, river, sister; bird, birthday, circle, first, girl, shirt, skirt, thirsty; church, fur, nurse, purple, purse, surprise, turn.*

DAY 1

Big Book 2B pp. 46–47; Pupil Book 2 pp. 38–39

Shared reading

- Read together the main heading and information on page 46. Can the children tell you whether the extract is fiction or non-fiction?
- Discuss the children's general opinion of snakes. Have any of the children handled a snake? Ask them to describe the feel of the snake's skin to the rest of the class. Talk about the snake's different senses.
- Can the children read the sub-heading on page 47 to you? Read page 47 together. Find out if any of the children have recently grown out of a pair of trousers or other item of clothing. Relate this to the snake's need to shed its skin as a result of growth.
- How long does it take a snake to shed its skin? Why does the snake hide when its eyes turn milky? How does the snake begin to shed its skin?

Focused word/sentence work

- Can the children find a colour on page 47 beginning with *wh*? Can they find two more words beginning with *wh* on this page (*why* (subheading) and *when*)?
- Read the phrase, "its eyes turn milky white" and write the word *turn* on the board, underlining *ur*. Now read the phrase "it hides away from danger" together and write the word *danger* on the board, underlining *er*. What do the children notice about the phonemes *ur* and *er* you have underlined (same sound, different spelling)? (Note that the pronunciation of the *er*, *ir* and *ur* phoneme varies regionally; please adapt the work on *er*, *ir* and *ur* in this unit as appropriate for your region.)
- Re-read the second paragraph on page 47, asking the children to listen out for other words containing the *er* phoneme as you do so (*first, turning, underneath*). How many syllables can the children hear in these words?

Independent work

- The questions on page 39 of Pupil Book 2 test children's understanding of the process of a snake shedding its skin.

Plenary

- Re-read page 46, asking the children to listen out for words containing the *er* phoneme (*whether, slither, terrific, expert*).

DAY 2

Big Book 2B pp. 47–48; Pupil Book 2 p. 39

Shared reading

- Re-read page 47 to reinforce the children's understanding of the process of a snake shedding its skin (in preparation for this week's shared writing activity).
- Ask the children to read the subheading on page 48 to you. Read the information on this page, pointing to the text as you do so. How many children knew that some snakes hatch from an egg like chicks? Talk about the special egg tooth. How many children have got wobbly teeth which they are about to lose?

Focused word/sentence work

- Re-read page 48 together, asking the children to listen for words containing the *er* phoneme (*birth, others, slithered*). Write *birth* on the board and underline *ir*. Give the children clues to other words containing the spelling pattern *ir* and write these on the board as the children guess them, e.g. *bird, birthday, circle, first, girl, shirt, skirt, thirsty*.
- Read through the words in the index from a book about snakes on page 39 of Pupil Book 2. Ask the children a couple of questions to prepare them for today's independent work, e.g. Which page would you turn to if you wanted to learn about cobras?

Independent work

- The children are required to answer questions on page 39 of Pupil Book 2 relating to the index you have just read together.

Plenary

- Look again at the subheading on page 48. Write the word *born* on the board and underline *or*. Listen to the sound of the vowel phoneme *or*. Give the children clues to other words containing the spelling pattern *or* and write them on the board as they are correctly guessed, e.g. *corner, forgive, horse, morning, popcorn, short, sport, storm, story, torch.*

DAY 3

Big Book 2B pp. 49–50; Pupil Book 2 p. 39

Shared reading

- Ask the children to read the sub-heading on page 49. Read pages 49 and 50, tracking the text for the children to follow. Discuss the meaning of any words which may be unfamiliar to the children, e.g. *venom.*
- Talk about the reason why a snake needs to kill other animals (for food). Can the children suggest creatures in the animal kingdom which eat snakes?

Focused word/sentence work

- Re-read the first two sentences on page 50. Write *curved* on the board and underline *ur*. Give clues to other words containing the spelling pattern *ur*, e.g. *burger, church, curtain, fur, furniture, nurse, purple, purse, surprise, turkey.* Can the children think of two days of the week that contain the spelling pattern *ur*?
- Ask the children to remind you of two other ways of spelling the *ur* phoneme (*er* and *ir*). Write an example of a word containing each spelling on the board and read them together.

Independent work

- Children who complete the exercises on page 39 of Pupil Book 2 within the given time could look in their own reading books for more words containing *er, ir* and *ur* and record them. Alternatively, they could practise using indexes in non-fiction books appropriate to their reading ability.

Plenary

- Hand out a selection of word cards with words containing *er, ir* and *ur*. Write the three different spellings of this phoneme on the board as headings. Ask the children, in turn, to read aloud their word and decide which of the three columns it should be recorded under. These words will be revised within Unit 19.

DAY 4

Pupil Book 2 p. 39; Copymaster 18

Shared writing

- Ask the children to tell you how a snake sheds its skin. Briefly write down the pieces of information they offer you in the order that they are given. (If the children are having difficulty remembering the process, refer back to page 47 in Big Book 2B.)
- Help the children to organise their information into a few simple sentences.

Focused word/sentence work

- Check that the sentences are sequenced and punctuated correctly. Are the children happy with the wording of their information?
- Emphasize that the clarity of the instructions is more important in this instance than effective vocabulary. The purpose of the writing is to inform.
- Give each child a copy of Copymaster 18. Discuss the presentation of the diagram which the children are about to complete. Explain that the information in this instance can be presented in a circular diagram rather than a list because the process of shedding skin is repeated as the snake continues to grow.

Independent work

- The children may complete the diagram on Copymaster 18, adding their own text and pictures as indicated.

Plenary

- Hand out the word cards with words containing *er, ir* and *ur* that you used on Day 3. Write the three different spellings of this phoneme on the board as headings. Ask the children, in turn to read aloud their word and decide which of the three columns it should be recorded under. Alternatively, you may like to pin the cards to a more permanent wall display so that they may be added to during the course of the term.

DAY 5

Big Book 2B pp. 49–50; Pupil Book 2 p. 39; Copymaster 18 from Day 4

Shared reading

- Re-read pages 49 and 50.

Focused word/sentence work

- Revise the term *digest.* Can the children show you which part of their bodies the jaw is? Write the word *jaw* on the board and underline *aw*. Give clues to other words containing the spelling pattern *aw*, e.g. *awful, crawl, draw, law, paw, saw, straw, yawn.*

Independent work

- The children should use this time to complete their diagrams. Children who finish within the twenty minutes could present information about something else that interested them about snakes during shared reading this week.

Plenary

- Construct a cyclical diagram together about a subject of your own choosing, e.g. the life-cycle of the frog.

Consolidation and extension

- Use Copymaster 1 to practise spelling words containing *er, ir, ur* and *or.*
- Begin a collection of information books about snakes and other reptiles. Compare the different ways in which similar information is presented.
- Make a class glossary of special interest words linked to the topic of snakes.

Homework

- Page 19 of Homework Book 2 provides practice of the common spelling patterns for the vowel phoneme *er/ir/ur*, focusing on words from this week's shared text.

Unit 19

Lao Lao of Dragon Mountain

Key Learning Objectives

TL3	to discuss and compare story themes
TL4	to predict story endings/incidents, e.g. from unfinished extracts, while reading with the teacher
TL5	discuss story settings to compare differences; to locate key words and phrases in text; to consider how different settings influence events and behaviour
TL6	to identify and describe characters, expressing own views and using words and phrases from texts
TL13	to use story settings from reading, e.g. re-describe, use in own writing, write a different story in the same setting
TL16	to use dictionaries to locate words by using initial letter
TL17	to learn that dictionaries give definitions and explanations; discuss what definitions are, explore some simple definitions in dictionaries
WL2	to learn the common spelling patterns for the vowel phoneme *er*
WL8	to spell words with common prefixes, e.g. *un-*, *dis-*, to indicate the negative
WL11	to learn the use of antonyms and collect and discuss differences of meaning and their spelling

Range:	Fiction and poetry: stories from other cultures; stories with patterned language
Texts:	From *Lao Lao of Dragon Mountain*, Margaret Bateson-Hill
Resources:	Big Book 2B pp. 51–58 Pupil Book 2 pp. 40–41 Copymasters 11 and 19 Homework Book 2 p. 20

Preparation

- Day 1: you will need a globe or world map.
- Day 2: you will need the word cards with words containing *er*, *ir* and *ur* that you prepared for Unit 18. If you did not use them as part of a word display, you will also need props or pictures of things containing *er*, *ir* and *ur* (a flower, a bird or shirt, and a church, nurse or purse).
- Day 5: the children will need dictionaries appropriate to their reading abilities.

DAY 1

Big Book 2B pp. 51–52; Pupil Book 2 pp. 40

Shared reading

- Introduce the story *Lao Lao of Dragon Mountain* by Margaret Bateson-Hill. Explain that this story comes from China. Show where this is in relation to Britain on a globe or world map. How many children have been to China? What can they tell you about the country?
- Read pages 51 and 52. Talk about the setting of this story.
- Do the children think that the Ice Dragon will turn out to be a friendly or a frightening dragon? Discuss the character of Lao Lao.
- Have any of the children made a paper-cut (a snowflake, for example)?

Focused word/sentence work

- Write the word *unfolded* on the board. Cover the prefix, *un-* and ask the children to read you the word that remains. Explain that *unfolded* is the opposite of *folded*. Can the children tell you the opposite of *comfortable*, *helpful*, *lock* and *pack*? Write these words on the board with the prefix *un-*.
- Look at page 51 together. Can the children find words that mean the opposite of *young* (*old*), *huge* (*tiny*), *inside* (*outside*), *back* (*front*), *close* (*open*)?

Independent work

- The questions on page 41 of Pupil Book 2 relate to the extract you have read together today.

Plenary

- Re-read pages 51 and 52 together.
- Help the children to learn Lao Lao's song by heart:
  "Fold it and cut it and turn it around
  Open it up and see what you've found."

DAY 2

Big Book 2B pp. 53–54; Pupil Book 2 p. 41

Shared reading

- Ask the children to re-tell the story of Lao Lao so far before reading page 53.
- Talk about the Emperor. Can the children predict what sort of role he will have to play in the story as it unfolds?
- Read page 54. What do they think will happen next?

Focused word/sentence work

- Can the children find three words next to each other on page 54, which begin with the same letters (*steep*, *stone*, *steps*)? Discuss whether or not the children think that the author has done this intentionally.
- Can the children identify the words spoken by the guards on page 54, using the speech marks?
- Write the following sentence on the board: *Lao Lao made paper butterflies and flowers.* Underline *er* in the word *paper* and ask the children to read the word and say the underlined sound. Can they find this sound anywhere else in your sentence? Ask volunteers to come and underline the sound in *butterflies* and *flowers*.
- Can the children remember any other ways of spelling the *er* sound (*ir* and *ur*)? (Note that the pronunciation of the *er*, *ir* and *ur* phoneme varies regionally; please adapt the work on *er*, *ir* and *ur* in this unit as appropriate for your region.) Can the children recall words containing these spelling patterns from Unit 18? If you made a display of these word families, refer to it now, asking

the children to read the words to you. Alternatively, hand out the word cards you prepared for Unit 18. Choose three children to stand at the front each holding a different picture (a flower, a bird or shirt, and a church, nurse or purse). Ask the children with the word cards to read aloud their word and give it to the child holding a prop or picture of something with the corresponding spelling pattern.

Independent work

- The exercises on page 41 of Pupil Book 2 revise words containing the spelling patterns *er*, *ir* and *ur*.

Plenary

- Re-read pages 53 and 54 together.

DAY 3

Big Book 2B pp. 56–58; Pupil Book 2 p. 41

Shared reading

- Recap on the story so far before reading pages 56 to 58. Have the children read any other stories about dragons like this one before? What are dragons said to breathe usually, rather than ice-cold breath?
- Do the children feel sorry for the Emperor and his guards? Discuss the magical ending to the story.

Focused word/sentence work

- Look at the sentence "Lao Lao grew colder and colder" on page 56. Discuss the function of *er* in the word *colder*. Write the following words on the board: *small, fast, slow*. Ask the children to read these words and tell you what they will become if you add *-er* to each. Add *-er* to each word and re-read them. How has the meaning of each word changed?
- Can the children find two other words ending in *-er* on page 56 (*paper* and *tower*)? Does *er* have the same function in these words?

Independent work

- Children use this time to complete the exercises on page 41 of Pupil Book 2.

Plenary

- Invite some of the children to read the sentences they have written containing words with *er*, *ir* or *ur*.

DAY 4

Pupil Book 2 p. 41; Copymaster 19

Shared writing

- Discuss the writing task outlined on page 41 of Pupil Book 2. Create a wordbank of vocabulary to describe the village and the mountain that provide the setting for the story. Refer to both the text and the illustrations to inspire the children to think of interesting adjectives and adjectival phrases.
- Help the children to select the best of their ideas and weave them into a descriptive passage about the story setting. Write the description in a way that it could be used to open a story.

Focused word/sentence work

- Check the punctuation of your writing together. Are the children completely happy with their choice of vocabulary? Would they like to add anything to the description (either based on evidence from the text or something original from their own imaginations).
- The children might like to close their eyes as you read their writing back to them. Are they able to visualise the story setting effectively from the description?

Independent work

- Using Copymaster 19, the children can begin writing their own description of the story setting using ideas developed within the shared writing session.

Plenary

- Choose children to read the beginning of their descriptions to the class. Encourage the rest of the class to identify the best features of each.

DAY 5

Big Book 2B pp. 56–58; Copymaster 19 from Day 4

Shared reading

- Re-read pages 56 to 58 together.

Focused word/sentence work

- Hand out dictionaries to the children and help them to locate the following words from pages 56 to 58 and read out the definition to the rest of the class: *dragon, palace, mountain, harvest*. If you have an alphabet frieze on the wall of your classroom, show where the initial letter of each word comes in the alphabet sequence to give the children an idea of where to find the word in their dictionaries.

Independent work

- The children may use this time to complete the descriptive writing they began on Day 4.

Plenary

- Choose different children to read their completed descriptions to the class. Encourage the class to comment on the most effective words and phrases from each.

Consolidation and extension

- Read the full story of *Lao Lao of Dragon Mountain* by Margaret Bateson-Hill. The story is written in Chinese alongside the English text.
- The children could write a new story set in the context of Lao Lao's village. The descriptive writing which the children produced on Days 4 and 5 could form the opening to their new stories.
- Use the passport template on Copymaster 11 to write a character profile of either Lao Lao or the Emperor.

Homework

- Page 20 of Homework Book 2 provides instructions for making a paper-cut butterfly like Lao Lao's for children to read and follow.

Unit 20 Badger's Parting Gifts

Key Learning Objectives

TL3	to discuss and compare story themes
TL5	to discuss story settings: to compare differences; to locate key words and phrases in text; to consider how different settings influence events and behaviour
TL6	to identify and describe characters, expressing own views and using words and phrases from texts
TL14	to write character profiles, e.g. simple descriptions, posters, passports, using key words and phrases that describe or are spoken by characters in the text
WL4	to split familiar oral and written compound words into their component parts
WL5	to discriminate, orally, syllables in multi-syllabic words using children's names and words from their reading. Extend to written forms and note syllable boundary in speech and writing
WL8	to spell words with common prefixes, e.g. *un-*, *dis-*, to indicate the negative
SL7	to investigate and recognise a range of other ways of presenting texts, e.g. speech bubbles, enlarged, bold or italicised print, captions, headings and sub-headings

Range:	Fiction: stories with predictable language
Texts:	From *Badger's Parting Gifts*, Susan Varley, Collins
Resources:	Big Book 2B pp. 59–64 Pupil Book 2 pp. 42–43 Copymaster 20 Assessment master, Term 2 Homework Book 2 p. 21

Preparation

- Days 3 and 5: prepare two different coloured sets of word cards, featuring the following words and any others of your own choosing – set A: *foot, light, news, sea, super, tea*; set B: *ball, house, paper, side, market, spoon*.

DAY 1

Big Book 2B pp. 59–64; Pupil Book 2 pp. 42–43

Shared reading

- Spend this session reading the entire extract from *Badger's Parting Gifts* to the children. The story deals with the issues of dying and grief and is best reflected upon as a whole.
- Consider the feelings of the animal friends Badger left behind. What were their memories of him?

Focused word/sentence work

- Look in detail at page 59. Read this page again, together, if time allows. Can the children find words to describe what sort of a character Badger was (*dependable, reliable, old*, etc.)?

Independent work

- The comprehension questions on page 43 of Pupil Book 2 relate to today's extract from *Badger's Parting Gifts*.

Plenary

- Ask the children what words they think their friends would use to describe them.
- What would the children say to the other animals to make them feel better?

DAY 2

Big Book 2B pp. 60–62; Pupil Book 2 p. 43

Shared reading

- Re-read pages 60 to 62 together. What was the weather like outside when Badger arrived home late? What was it like inside his underground home? What did Badger do when he had finished his supper?
- Talk about the events of the following day. Who read Badger's note to the other animals? How did they feel?

Focused word/sentence work

- Ask the class to turn to page 43 in Pupil Book 2. Read through the explanation together. List other words, e.g. *lucky, safe, tie*. Ask the children to tell you what these words would become if you added the prefix *un-*. Write out each word with the prefix *un-*.
- Repeat this activity for words with the prefix *dis-*, e.g. *disagree, disapprove*. Explain how the prefixes *un-* and *dis-* change a word, e.g. *to disagree* means that you *do not* agree.

Independent work

- Exercise A on page 43 of Pupil Book 2 reinforces understanding of the prefixes *dis-* and *un-*.

Plenary

- The children may like to talk about things which make them feel unhappy. End on a positive note by discussing the things which make them feel happy.

DAY 3

Big Book 2B pp. 60, 63–64; Pupil Book 2 p. 43

Shared reading

- Re-read the conclusion to the story extract on pages 63 and 64 together. What time of year is it now? What time of year was it when Badger died (look for evidence in the text at the bottom of page 60)? How much time has passed?
- Can the children think of any other animal stories which are set in the countryside?
- Find out how many children can do each of the things that Badger taught his animal friends to do. Can the children think of things that their friends or relations have taught them how to do, e.g. ride a bike?
- Do the children think Badger's friends will ever forget him? Why?

Focused word/sentence work

- Write the word *gingerbread* on the board. Show how it is made up of two smaller words by covering each in turn and asking the class to read the word that remains. Repeat this exercise using other compound words, e.g. *football, lighthouse, newspaper, seaside*. Ask the children to tell you how many syllables they can hear in each compound word. Can the class think of any other examples?

Independent work

- The exercise on page 43 of Pupil Book 2 requires children to split compound words into their component parts.

Plenary

- Hand out set A of the word cards (see **Preparation**) to a group of children and ask them to stand at the front of the class. Give the second set out to children who are still sitting. Ask the children at the front of the class to read their words in turn. As each child reads his or her word, the children with a word from set B should check to see if their word can be added to the first to make a compound word. He or she then joins the relevant child at the front and they read their new word together.

DAY 4

Pupil Book 2 p. 43; Copymaster 20

Shared writing

- Talk about the writing activity on page 43 of Pupil Book 2. Ask the children to think of words and phrases to describe Badger, taking into account his appearance, his character and special talents. Write down the children's ideas on a board or flip chart, for them to refer to during their independent work.
- What did the other animals like best about Badger?
- Help the children write a profile of Badger using the ideas they have contributed.

Focused word/sentence work

- Focus on the organisation of the shared writing. Is there too much information for one poster? Decide collectively on what should be cut and what should remain. Have the children chosen the most effective adjectives to describe Badger?
- Discuss different ways of presenting text on a poster, using a range a presentational devices, e.g. speech bubbles, enlarged or bold print, captions, headings and sub-headings. Which of these might be appropriate on the children's posters?

Independent work

- Using Copymaster 20, the children can produce their own posters about Badger for his friends to remember him by. You may prefer them to draft the text on ordinary paper today and use Copymaster 20 to present their checked, redrafted writing, in best handwriting on Day 5.

Plenary

- Invite a few of the children to read their character profiles to the rest of the class. In each case, highlight the most successful aspects of the writing.

DAY 5

Big Book 2B pp. 63–64; Copymaster 20 from Day 4

Shared reading

- Re-read pages 63 and 64. Ask the children to talk about occasions when they have taught a younger brother or sister or a friend how to do something. Which of the skills that Badger taught his friends would they most like to learn?

Focused word/sentence work

- Repeat the game you played with the class during the plenary session on Day 3, using the cards featuring the component parts of compound words.

Independent work

- The children should use this time to complete their character profiles of Badger on Copymaster 20.

Plenary

- Invite different children to read their completed character profiles to the rest of the class. Encourage the class to talk about the best features of each.

Consolidation and extension

- Read the full story of *Badger's Parting Gifts* by Susan Varley.
- The children could write a letter to a friend or relative saying what they admire most about them.
- The Assessment master for Term 2 provides revision of teaching points covered this term as a means of assessing children's progress.

Homework

- Page 21 of Homework Book 2 focuses on compound words.

TERM 3

HALF-TERMLY PLANNER

Year 2 • Term 3 • Weeks 1–5

SCHOOL ____________________ **CLASS** ________ **TEACHER** ______________

		Phonetics, spelling and vocabulary	Grammar and punctuation	Comprehension and composition	Texts
Continuous work **Weeks 1–5**		WL 1, 4, 5, 8, 11, 12	SL 1, 5	1, 2, 9	**Range** **Fiction and poetry:** extended stories, stories by significant children's authors; different stories by the same author; texts with language play, e.g. riddles, tongue-twisters, humorous verse and stories **Non-fiction:** information books including non-chronological reports
Blocked work **Week**	**Unit**				**Titles**
1	**21**	WL 7	SL 3	TL 10	From *The Pudding Like a Night on the Sea* in *The Julian Stories*, Ann Cameron
2	**22**	WL 10	SL 3	TL 3	From *The Worst Witch*, Jill Murphy
3	**23**	WL 3, 6	SL 4, 6	TL 5, 14, 21	From *Author Profile*, Book Trust: Jill Murphy; From *Author Profile*, Book Trust: Dick King-Smith
4	**24**	WL 2, 3, 6, 7		TL 3, 4, 8, 13, 16, 17, 18, 19, 21	From *The Hodgeheg*, Dick King-Smith
5	**25**	WL 9	SL 6, 7	TL 13, 14, 15, 16, 17, 18, 19, 20, 21	*The Nation's Favourite Game*; From *Soccer Star*, Michael Hardcastle

TERM 3

HALF-TERMLY PLANNER

Year 2 • Term 3 • Weeks 6–10

SCHOOL ____________ **CLASS** ________ **TEACHER** ____________

		Phonetics, spelling and vocabulary	Grammar and punctuation	Comprehension and composition	Texts
Continuous work Weeks 6–10		WL 1, 4, 5, 8, 11, 12	SL 1, 5	TL 1, 2, 9	**Range** **Fiction and poetry**: extended stories, stories by significant children's authors; different stories by the same author; texts with language play, e.g. riddles, tongue-twisters, humorous verse and stories **Non-fiction**: information books including non-chronological reports
Blocked work **Week**	**Unit**				**Titles**
6	**26**	WL 10	SL 3	TL 3, 10	From *Fangs*, Malorie Blackman
7	**27**	WL 2, 3		TL 6, 8, 11	From *Laughter is an Egg*, John Agard; From *Riddles and Rhymes and Rigmaroles*, John Cunliffe; *Betty Botter . . .*, Traditional
8	**28**	WL 10	SL 2	TL 6, 7, 8, 11	*Brother*, Mary Ann Hoberman; From *Press Play*, Anne Fine
9	**29**	WL 2, 9	SL 4	TL 13, 15, 16, 20, 21	*How do we Communicate?*; *Helen Keller*
10	**30**	WL 3, 10		TL 3, 6, 7, 8, 10, 12	From *Revolting Rhymes*, Roald Dahl

Unit 21

The Pudding Like a Night on the Sea

Key Learning Objectives

TL10 to write sustained stories, using knowledge of story elements: narrative, settings, characterisation, dialogue and the language of story

WL7 to spell words with common suffixes, e.g. *-ful, -ly*

SL3 to use standard forms of verbs in speaking and writing, e.g. *catch/caught, see/saw, go/went* and to use the past tense consistently for narration

Range:	Fiction and poetry: extended stories; stories by significant children's authors
Texts:	From *The Pudding Like a Night on the Sea* in *The Julian Stories*, Ann Cameron
Resources:	Big Book 2C pp. 4–9 Pupil Book 2 pp. 44–45 Copymaster 21 Homework Book p. 22

DAY 1

Big Book 2C pp. 4–7; Pupil Book 2 pp. 44–45

Shared reading

- Introduce today's story extract, *The Pudding Like a Night on the Sea* by Ann Cameron. How many children have heard or read any of *The Julian Stories*?
- Read through pages 4 to 6 together. How many of the children have helped make a pudding or cake at home?
- Do the children think that Huey and Julian will be able to resist touching the pudding while their father is asleep? Read page 7 to find out.

Focused word/sentence work

- How many syllables can the children hear in the names Julian and Huey?
- Refer back to the stages involved in making the pudding and write each step on the board as though producing a set of instructions, e.g.:

  Slice five lemons in half.
  Squeeze each lemon half.
  Crack some eggs and put the yolks into a pan and the whites into a bowl.
  Beat the egg yolks . . .
- Note the difference in tense of the verbs in the instruction writing from the past tense typical of narrative.

Independent work

- The questions on page 45 of Pupil Book 2 relate to today's story extract.

Plenary

- Re-read the instructions on the board together and think of a mime for each action. Revise the teaching points of Unit 9 in Term 1 relating to instructional text, e.g. use of direct language.

DAY 2

Big Book 2C pp. 7–9; Pupil Book 2 p. 45

Shared reading

- Re-read page 7 together before reading pages 8 and 9. Why do the children think Julian and Huey ran to their bedroom and crawled under their bed? What do they think will happen next? What will their father have to say when he awakes?

Focused word/sentence work

- Turn back to page 7. Read Huey's words: "Oh, it's a wonderful pudding." Write the word *wonderful* on the board and explain its meaning (*full of wonder*). Challenge the children to think of other words ending in the suffix *-ful* and write each one on the board, e.g. *beautiful, careful, dreadful, painful*. Cover *-ful* in each word and read the word that remains. Note that the *y* in *beauty* changes to an *i* in *beautiful*. Explain that this happens to words that end in *-y* when the suffix *-ful* is added.

Independent work

- The exercises on page 45 of Pupil Book 2 for Days 2 and 3 focus on the suffix *-ful*.

Plenary

- Ask the children to read the words they have made by adding the suffix *-ful* to the words on page 45 of Pupil Book 2. Challenge them to make up sentences orally that include these words.

DAY 3

Big Book 2C pp. 7–9; Pupil Book 2 p. 45

Shared reading

- Re-read pages 7 to 9 together.
- Encourage the children to discuss occasions when they have touched something they were asked not to. What was it that they were not supposed to touch? What were the consequences of their actions? Discuss adults' reasons for asking a child not to touch something, e.g. because it's dangerous, because it's fragile.

Focused word/sentence work

- What is a "raft"? Can the children explain to you what "craters on the moon" are?
- Divide the class into two and re-read the dialogue on page 7 with half the class reading Huey's words and the rest reading Julian's words. Guide the children through this task by pointing to the dialogue. Discuss the function of the speech marks in indicating the spoken words.

Independent work

- Exercise B on page 45 of Pupil Book 2 requires the children to contextualise words ending in the suffix *-ful* within sentences of their own (remind them of the Plenary session on Day 2).

Plenary

- Explore possible outcomes of the story extract through role-play. What will the boys have to say to their father? What will he say to them?

DAY 4

Pupil Book 2 p. 45; Copymaster 21

Shared writing

- Introduce the writing challenge set out on page 45 of Pupil Book 2. What sort of surprise might Julian and Huey plan for their father? Discuss the ideas put forward by the class and decide upon one to explore through shared writing.
- Help the children turn their ideas into a piece of story writing, using the formal elements of the story extract. Introduce the characters before detailing the planned surprise.
- Discuss whether the surprise will run smoothly as planned. Point out that the story might be more interesting to read if the boys encounter a problem or setback of some kind.
- Will there be a happy ending? What will Julian and Huey's father think of their efforts to surprise him?

Focused word/sentence work

- Help the pupils organise their ideas effectively in the past tense. Identify a clear beginning, middle and conclusion to the story.
- Introduce the story planner on Copymaster 21. Talk through the questions posed with the children.

Independent work

- Using Copymaster 21 the children may plan their own stories, developing the ideas you have discussed together. Children who complete this within the time allowed could begin to write their own story using the plan to help them organise their writing effectively.

Plenary

- Invite a few of the children to talk about how they answered the questions on their plans. Discuss how the children can use their plans to help them write their own stories.

DAY 5

Big Book 2C pp. 4–9; Copymaster 21 from Day 4

Shared reading

- Re-read the extract from *The Pudding Like a Night on the Sea* in its entirety.

Focused word/sentence work

- Revise the suffix, *-ful*. Give the children clues to words ending in *-ful*, e.g. *if someone has a bad memory they are . . .* (*forgetful*). Write each word on the board and underline *-ful*.
- Choose some of the examples on the board to show how the suffix *-ly* can be added, e.g. *carefully*. Ask the class to give you a sentence using this word.
- Extend this work by introducing the suffix *-ly*. Explain that *-ly* can be added to some but not all of the examples on the board. Point out that most words ending in *-ful* and/or *-ly* are describing words, and give examples of each.

Independent work

- Use this time to complete the story writing started on Day 4. Many children may need additional time to complete their stories outside the literacy hour.

Plenary

- Invite some of the children to read their story writing to the class. Check that the stories are written consistently in the past tense. Highlight any grammatical errors and see if the rest of the class are able to correct these orally.

Consolidation and extension

- Read more of *The Julian Stories* by Ann Cameron.
- Create a wordbank of adjectives and adverbs ending in *-ful* and *-ly*, and encourage the children to begin to introduce more of these words into their own writing (it is not necessary for them to know the terms "adjective" and "adverb" at this stage).

Homework

- Page 22 of Homework Book 2 provides further reinforcement of the suffixes *-ful* and *-ly*.

Unit 22

The Worst Witch

Key Learning Objectives

TL3 to notice the difference between spoken and written forms through re-telling known stories comparing oral versions with the written text

WL10 to use synonyms and other alternative words/ phrases that express same or similar meanings; to collect and discuss similarities and shades of meaning to extend and enhance writing

SL3 to use standard forms of verbs in speaking and writing, e.g. *catch/caught, see/saw, go/went* and to use the past tense consistently for narration

Range:	Fiction and poetry: extended stories; stories by significant children's authors
Texts:	From *The Worst Witch*, Jill Murphy
Resources:	Big Book 2C pp. 10–14 Pupil Book 2 pp. 46–47 Copymaster 22 Homework Book 2 p. 23

Preparation

- Days 1 and 3: make a set of word cards featuring pairs of synonyms, with one word on each card, e.g. *wet/damp; angry/cross; big/large; mean/unkind; fast/quick.*

DAY 1

Big Book 2C pp. 10–12; Pupil Book 2 pp. 46–47

Shared reading

- The story extract on pages 10 to 14 is from *The Worst Witch*, the first in a series of books about Mildred Hubble by Jill Murphy. Read page 10 with the children. What happens when Mildred puts her kitten on the broomstick?
- Read pages 11 and 12. Ask the children to explain how Mildred got her kitten to stay on the broomstick. What do they think of her idea?

Focused word/sentence work

- Turn back to page 10. Can the children think of a word that is similar in meaning (in the context of this extract) to each of the following: *trouble, attempts, severely?*
- Look at page 11 together. Consider alternative words, similar in meaning to the following: *gazed, sadly, angry, hard.*

Independent work

- Ask the children to answer the questions on page 47 of Pupil Book 2, relating to today's fiction extract.

Plenary

- Hand out word cards featuring synonyms (see **Preparation**). Ask one child at a time to read out his or her word card. The child with a word similar in meaning to that which has just been read out should raise his or her hand, read the word and join the other child. Once all the children with word cards have paired up, ask one of each pair to read their word and see if the rest of the class are able to recall the other word which is similar in meaning. Can the class think of any other words similar to those which have been read?

DAY 2

Big Book 2C pp. 12–14; Pupil Book 2 p. 47

Shared reading

- Re-read page 12 together before reading pages 13 and 14.
- Look at the reference to a distance of "ten feet" on page 13. Ask the children to show you with their hands how long they think a foot is.
- What does Miss Hardbroom mean by "it would be even easier with handlebars and a saddle"?
- What opinion do the children have of Miss Hardbroom? Help them to justify their comments by referring back to specific phrases in the text that provide clues about her character, e.g. "an icy voice"; "stony glare".

Focused word/sentence work

- Read the first sentence on page 12. Write the word *school* on the board. What do the children notice about the spelling of this word? Underline *ch* and ask the children to tell you the sound of this digraph. Give clues to other words containing *ch* as in *school*, e.g. *chemist, Christmas, choir, headache, stomach.*
- Point out the use of past tense verbs on pages 11 and 12, reminding the class that stories are usually told in the past tense, e.g. "the kitten fell"; "Mildred dived into the school"; "She came out carrying her satchel"; "Mildred flew delightedly round the yard". Can the children tell you what each of these verbs would be in the present tense? (It is not necessary for the children to use the term "verb" at this stage.)

Independent work

- Exercise A on page 47 of Pupil Book 2 gives practice of writing verbs in the past tense, using verbs that the children have met in today's shared text.

Plenary

- Re-read pages 12–14.

DAY 3

Big Book 2C pp. 10–12; Pupil Book 2 p. 47

Shared reading

- Re-read pages 10 to 12, focusing on the character of Mildred Hubble. As the children find evidence in the text about Mildred, make notes on a board or flipchart (you will refer to these notes again on Day 4), e.g. *Mildred had difficulty learning to ride her broomstick.*

Focused word/sentence work

- Repeat the game you played during the Plenary session on Day 1 using a set of word cards featuring synonyms (see **Preparation**).

- Can the class suggest when it may be necessary to think of a word which has the same or similar meaning (e.g. to avoid overuse of particular words; to add variety to a piece of writing)?

Independent work

- The class may use this time to complete the exercises on page 47 of Pupil Book 2, focusing on distinguishing past tense verbs.
- Give sentences in the present tense asking the children to repeat them, using the past tense.

DAY 4

Pupil Book 2 p. 47; Copymaster 22

Shared writing

- Read through the writing activity outlined on page 47 of Pupil Book 2. Refer back to the notes you made on Day 3 and decide how much of the evidence you gathered should be included in your writing.
- Talk about the title of the book from which this extract was taken. *The Worst Witch*. In what way is Mildred Hubble the "Worst Witch", do the children think?

Focused word/sentence work

- Use this time to redraft the ideas you have focused upon, to produce a simple character profile of Mildred Hubble. Talk about the sequence in which the information should appear, e.g. 1) Introduce her by name. 2) Explain that she attends a school for witches. 3) Mention that she has a friend called Maud and a kitten. Once the main facts have been established, the children may like to add further information and some of their own opinions about Mildred.
- Discuss whether or not the children have been repetitive in their choice of vocabulary. Refer back to your work on synonyms, and discuss whether any of the repeated or uninteresting words could be changed to something similar in meaning.
- Check the punctuation of the shared writing together.

Independent work

- The children can use this time to begin writing a character profile of Mildred Hubble. Copymaster 22 provides a writing frame for a character profile which includes a wordbank of adjectives to help children select appropriate vocabulary. Remind children using this sheet that not all the vocabulary will be appropriate and they must select words carefully when writing their description of Mildred. More able children may prefer to adopt their own format for producing a character profile.

Plenary

- Invite a few children to read their character profiles to the rest of the class. Talk about ways in which each of these could be developed further on Day 5.

DAY 5

Big Book 2C pp. 12–14; Copymaster 22 from Day 4

Shared reading

- Ask the class to retell the story extract now that they are more familiar with the storyline. Make notes of their oral version to refer to during the focused/word sentence work session.

Focused word/sentence work

- Re-read the second half of the extract from *The Worst Witch* on pages 12 to 14. Referring to the notes you made, compare the children's oral version of the story extract with the written text. Highlight the formal elements of story-telling and the rich use of vocabulary in the text.

Independent work

- The children should aim to complete their profile of Mildred Hubble during this session.

Plenary

- Choose different children to read their completed character profiles to the class.

Consolidation and extension

- Find out more about Mildred Hubble and her fellow pupils by reading other stories from *The Worst Witch*.
- Make collections of synonyms. Begin by making a wordbank of alternatives to *said*, e.g. *argued, asked, cried, enquired, replied, shouted, whispered, yelled.*

Homework

- Page 23 in Homework Book 2 provides practice in recognising synonyms.

Unit 23 Meet the Writers

Key Learning Objectives

TL5 to read about authors from information on book covers, e.g. other books written, whether the author is alive or dead, publisher; to become aware of authorship and publication

TL14 to pose questions and record these in writing, prior to reading non-fiction to find answers

TL21 to write non-chronological reports based on structure of known texts

WL3 to discriminate, spell and read the phonemes *ear* (as in *hear*) and *ea* (as in *head*)

WL6 to investigate words which have the same spelling patterns but different sounds

SL4 to use commas in lists

SL6 to turn statements into questions, learning a range of *wh* words typically used to open questions: *what, where, when, who* and to add question marks

Range:	Non-fiction: non-chronological reports
Texts:	From *Author Profile*, Book Trust: Jill Murphy From *Author Profile*, Book Trust: Dick King-Smith
Resources:	Big Book 2C pp. 15–20 Pupil Book 2 pp. 48–49 Copymaster 23 Homework Book 2 p. 24

DAY 1

Big Book 2C pp. 15–16; Pupil Book 2 pp. 48–49

Shared reading

- Are the children able to tell you who wrote the story of *The Worst Witch*?
- Hand out a slip of paper to each child and ask them to write down something they would be interested to know about Jill Murphy, in the form of a question.
- Read page 15. What was the first book that Jill Murphy had published?
- Read page 16. Point out that Jill Murphy illustrates her own books. Do all the children understand the meaning of the word *illustrate*? Can the children name another book written and illustrated by Jill Murphy, which is referred to on page 16? Do they know the titles of any other books by her?
- How many children have now had their question about Jill Murphy answered? If they have not found the answer to their question, where else might they look to learn more about a particular author (e.g. on the cover of a book by them)?

Focused word/sentence work

- Looking at the questionnaire on page 16, ask the children to read you the word that begins three of the questions. Write the word *what* on the board and underline *wh*. Can the class think of other words often used to begin questions (suggest that they refer to the questions they wrote on their slips of paper), e.g. *how, when, where, who, why*? How many of these words begin with *wh-*?

Independent work

- Ask the children to use today's extract to find answers to the questions posed on page 49 of Pupil Book 2.

Plenary

- Read pages 15 and 16 again. Is the extract fiction or non-fiction? What about *The Worst Witch*?

DAY 2

Big Book 2C pp. 17–19; Pupil Book 2 p. 49

Shared reading

- Dick King-Smith will probably need very little introduction as a celebrated children's writer. How many stories or books can the children think of that were written by him? Can they remember reading anything by him in Big Book 2B (*The Princess and the Pig* and an extract from *All Pigs are Beautiful*)?
- Read page 17. What does Dick King-Smith write about mostly?
- Read on to the end of the list of animals at the top of page 19. Discuss the writing process described by Dick King-Smith. How many children have often found themselves staring out of a window, with a blank sheet of paper in front of them, unable to think of a good idea for a story?

Focused word/sentence work

- Re-read the first sentence on page 18 together. Write the word *nearly* on the board. Can the children think of a word that means the same (*almost*)? Point out the *-ly* suffix. How many smaller words can the children find hidden within the word *nearly* (*near, ear, early*)?
- Focus on the word *ear*. Give clues to other words which contain this phoneme, and write them on the board as each is correctly guessed. Ask the children to help you spell each word, e.g. *clear, dear, fear, hear, near, tear*. Note that *deer* and *here* sound the same as *dear* and *hear* but are spelt differently and have different meanings. Do the children know the different meanings of these words? Note also that *tear* can be pronounced in two different ways, to give two different meanings.

Independent work

- Exercise A on page 49 of Pupil Book 2 asks the pupils to decide who they consider to be their favourite author. They are then asked to think of five questions to ask of him or her. Remind the class to end each question with a question mark.

Plenary

- Carry out a class survey of the children's favourite authors. Who is the overall favourite in your class?
- Ask different children to read out the questions they would like to ask their favourite authors.

DAY 3

Big Book 2C pp. 18–20; Pupil Book 2 p. 49

Shared reading

- Read pages 18 and 19. How many children enjoy reading stories about animals? Ask them to name a few of their favourites. What do the children think about Dick King-Smith's crossings-out and scribbles? Talk about the redrafting process.
- Read page 20. What does "scrawled" mean? What do "publishers" do? What does Dick King-Smith mean by "jacket"? What does he consider to be the "nicest thing of all" about writing for children?

Focused word/sentence work

- Talk about the commas and their purpose in the list of animals at the top of page 19. Write a few lists on the board and show where the commas should go. Make lists of the children's favourite animals, pets, colours, favourite authors, etc. and ask them to tell you where commas are needed.

Independent work

- Children who finish the exercises on page 49 of Pupil Book 2 could practise using commas within lists of their own.

Plenary

- Reflect upon Dick King-Smith's approach to creative writing. Ask the children to talk about how *they* approach story writing. Where do they get their ideas from? Do they like to spend time thinking through their ideas before they start writing? Do they prefer to write on paper or on a computer?
- How many children write stories or poems for fun at home? Do they work in a different way at home from the way they work at school? Where do they like to do their writing?

DAY 4

Pupil Book 2 p. 49

Shared writing

- Talk about the writing challenge on page 49 of Pupil Book 2. Help the children to devise a writing frame to use when carrying out the task independently. Discuss different ways of beginning sentences to put across the information that is asked for, e.g: *I like to write stories/poems about . . .; I like to write non-fiction about. . .; The best story I have ever written was called. . .; I begin a new story by. . .; My favourite place for writing is. . .* Write down the sentence openers you decide upon on a board or flip chart (The children will probably need to refer to them again on Day 5).

Focused word/sentence work

- Choose different children to complete each sentence orally. Write down the sentence endings for one of the children. Talk about the organisation and presentation of the writing.

Independent work

- The children should now be ready to write a "writer profile" about themselves independently, using the sentence openers you have agreed upon together. Challenge more able children to think of other ways to begin their sentences and other pieces of information to include.

Plenary

- Invite a few of the children to read their own writer profiles so far. Discuss what other information they may like to add to their writing on Day 5.

DAY 5

Big Book 2C pp. 15–16

Shared reading

- Re-read the author profile of Jill Murphy on pages 15 and 16. What does this profile have that the extract about Dick King-Smith does not (a questionnaire)?

Focused word/sentence work

- Compose together a set of questions for a questionnaire (things that the children would like to know about their favourite authors).

Independent work

- Pupils who finish their independent writing within the given time may like to try answering some of the questions you have written together about themselves.

Plenary

- Choose different children to read aloud their completed profiles.

Consolidation and extension

- Copymaster 23 provides a template for constructing a Question Wheel. The wheel will be most effective if constructed onto thin card. Children may find it useful to refer to their wheel when trying to think of, or spell, a question opener beginning with *wh-*.
- Give the children an opportunity to produce their own questionnaires which may then be answered by a friend.

Homework

- Page 24 in Homework Book 2 focuses on *ear* as in *hear* and as in *bear*.

Unit 24 The Hodgeheg

Key Learning Objectives

TL3	to notice the difference between spoken and written forms through re-telling known stories: compare oral versions with the written text
TL4	to compare books by the same author: settings, characters, themes; to evaluate and form preferences, giving reasons
TL8	to discuss meanings of words and phrases that create humour
TL13	to understand the distinction between fact and fiction; to use the terms *fact, fiction* and *non-fiction* appropriately
TL16	to scan a text to find specific sections, e.g. key words or phrases, subheadings
TL17	to skim-read title, contents page, illustrations, chapter headings and sub-headings, to speculate what a book might be about
TL18	to evaluate the usefulness of a text for its purpose
TL19	to make simple notes from non-fiction texts, e.g. key words and phrases, page references, headings, to use in subsequent writing
TL21	to write non-chronological reports based on structure of known texts
WL2	to reinforce work on discriminating syllables in reading and spelling from previous term
WL3	to discriminate, spell and read the phoneme *ea* (as in *head*)
WL6	to investigate words which have the same spelling patterns but different sounds
WL7	to spell words with common suffixes, e.g. *-ful, -ly*

Range:	Fiction and poetry: extended stories; stories by significant children's authors; different stories by the same author; texts with language play
Texts:	From *The Hodgeheg,* Dick King-Smith
Resources:	Big Book 2C pp. 21–31 Pupil Book 2 pp. 50–51 Homework Book 2 p. 25

Preparation

- Day 3: make available a selection of non-fiction texts for children to begin researching hedgehogs independently.

DAY 1

Big Book 2C pp. 21–23; Pupil Book 2 pp. 50–51

Shared reading

- Introduce *The Hodgeheg* by Dick King-Smith. Can the children remember reading other extracts from his books (*The Princess and the Pig* and *All Pigs are Beautiful*)?
- Read page 21 together. What happened to Auntie Betty?
- Read pages 22 and 23. How do humans cross the road safely? What advice would the children give Max?
- Can the children think of other names for Ma and Pa, e.g. *Mum, Mother, Mom, Mummy; Dad, Father, Pop, Daddy?*

Focused word/sentence work

- Reinforce work on discriminating syllables from the previous term. Ask the children to tell you how many syllables they can hear in the words *newsagent, road, nowadays, traffic, Max.* Cover each syllable in turn and demonstrate how this can be used as a strategy for spelling. Tackle the spelling of words such as *out/side, gar/den, prob/lems* and *safe/ly* by focusing on one syllable at a time together. Check the spelling of these words against the text on pages 22 and 23.
- Focus on the suffix *-ly* in the word *safely.* Explain that words ending in *-ly* usually explain how something is done, e.g. crossing the road safely, singing beautifully, munching crisps loudly. Ask the class to give further examples. Write down the adverb in each sentence that is offered and underline the *-ly* ending.

Independent work

- Ask the children to answer the comprehension questions relating to today's extract on page 51 of Pupil Book 2.

Plenary

- Re-read pages 21 to 23 and discuss what may happen next.

DAY 2

Big Book 2C pp. 24–27; Pupil Book 2 p. 51

Shared reading

- Read page 24 together. What is the "evening rush-hour"? Why is traffic especially busy at this time of day? At what other time of day is traffic likely to be as busy? What different forms of transport did Max observe?
- Read page 25. What is the "raised road" that Max referred to? What are the "noisy monsters"?
- Read pages 26 and 27. What has Max found? What do the children think will happens if Max crosses here in front of a lorry or car?

Focused word/sentence work

- Write the words spoken by Ma at the beginning of the extract on the board: "The traffic's dreadful". Underline *ea* in *dreadful.* What is the sound you have underlined? Talk about how this sound differs from *ea* in *eat.* Write the following words on the board: *bread, breakfast, deaf, feather, head, heavy, ready, weather.* Give a clue to each word and ask the children to find the word that you are referring to, e.g. something you use to make a sandwich; the first meal of the day.

Independent work

- The exercises on page 51 of Pupil Book 2 focus on the phoneme *ea* as in *bread.*

Plenary

- Look again at the word *dreadful*. Note the suffix, *-ful*. Can the children think of any other words ending in *-ful*, e.g. *careful, forgetful, painful, thoughtful, useful, wonderful*? (Remind them of the work they did in Unit 21.) Talk about the way in which words ending in *-ly* or *-ful* can be used to improve writing.
- Give the children a few very simple sentences to improve by adding a word ending in *-ly* or *-ful*, e.g. "the boy chose a card for his gran" could become "the *thoughtful* boy chose a *lovely* card for his gran".

DAY 3

Big Book 2C pp. 27–29; Pupil Book 2 p. 51

Shared reading

- Re-read page 27 together before reading page 28. What is a "pedestrian"? What does "straddle" mean? What is a "wing-mirror" and what is its function?
- Read page 29. Talk about how Max must be feeling after his series of shocks and a bump on the head. Discuss the meaning of any words which may be unfamiliar, e.g. *rump, catapaulted, dazedly*.

Focused word/sentence work

- Look at the words on page 28 with the prefix *un-*: *unaware, unhurt*. Talk about the negative function of *un-* which gives these words opposite meaning.
- Discuss the compound words *hedgehog* and those on pages 28 and 29: *something, halfway, headache*.

Independent work

- Children who finish the exercises on page 51 of Pupil Book 2 may like to scan appropriate non-fiction books for information about hedgehogs.

Plenary

- Give the children who have been looking for information about hedgehogs an opportunity to feed back their findings to the class.
- Draw the children's attention to important features in a non-fiction text about animals/hedgehogs: title, contents page, illustrations, chapter headings, sub-headings, captions, index, etc.

DAY 4

Pupil Book 2 p. 51

Shared writing

- Discuss the writing task outlined on page 51 of Pupil Book 2. Listen to all the children's ideas about road safety, making notes on a board or flip chart as you do so (thereby modelling the process of note-making).
- Decide, as a class, which of the ideas that have been suggested are the most important.

Focused word/sentence work

- Talk about the different ways of presenting information on a poster, e.g. speech bubbles, enlarged, bold or italicised print, captions, etc. Model some of the ways that you consider appropriate for this task.
- Discuss the design for your poster; where each of the ideas selected is to go and how they will be presented. Remind the children that both text and illustrations need to be relatively large and clear. Draw out a plan for a poster on a board or flip chart in response to the children's suggestions.
- Talk about the plan for a poster that you have produced collectively. What works best and what may need rethinking? How does this way of presenting information differ from other types of writing?

Independent work

- The children should work on a plan for their road safety posters which they will then reassess and use on Day 5.

Plenary

- Give the children time to look at a partner's plan. Ask them to point out the best features in their partner's work and make possible suggestions for improvements they think necessary. Invite one or two of the children to show their work to the class and tell the class what their partner liked best about it.

DAY 5

Big Book 2C pp. 21–31

Shared reading

- Ask the children to re-tell the story of *The Hodgeheg* so far. Compare their oral versions with the written texts, drawing on examples of specific formal story-telling language used by Dick King-Smith.
- Read the conclusion to the story extract on pages 30-31. Talk about the humour that arises from Max's muddled speech.

Focused word/sentence work

- Revise your teaching points about the phoneme *ea* as in *head*. How many words can the children remember? Challenge volunteers to come and write each word that is recalled.
- Write a few simple sentences on the board and ask the children to look for opportunities to add descriptive words ending in *-ful* or *-ly*. Point out that some words can have both endings, e.g. *she sang beautifully*.

Independent work

- The children may use this time to produce their final road safety posters, responding to the comments raised by their partners on Day 4.

Plenary

- Spend some time looking at the children's posters together. Discuss the accuracy of the advice given about road safety. Draw attention to the best advice. Who has presented the information on their poster most clearly?
- Play with other animal names in the way that Dick King-Smith has played with "hodgeheg", e.g. *champinzee, flimango, hoppopitamus*.

Consolidation and extension

- Like Jill Murphy's *The Worst Witch, The Hodgeheg* by Dick King-Smith is an extended story. Read the class more chapters from this short novel about Max's search for a safe place to cross and find out if his muddled speech returns to normal.
- Provide the children with a range of non-fiction books to find out more about hedgehogs. Encourage them to evaluate the usefulness of each text for this task. Alert them to the need to look at the title, contents page, illustrations, chapter headings and sub-headings. More able children could be given a more specific task, e.g. find out more about hibernation. They may need to be shown how to scan text to find specific information.
- Spend time comparing different texts by Dick King-Smith in greater detail, focusing on settings, characters and themes. Encourage the children to form, and give reasons for, their preferences.

Homework

- Page 25 of Homework Book 2 provides a non-fiction text about hedgehogs from which the children are asked to make simple notes. These notes could be used in subsequent writing. Suggest that children begin by reading the note headings and underline key words as they read through the information.

Unit 25

Football Crazy

Key Learning Objectives

TL13 to understand the distinction between fact and fiction; to use the terms *fact, fiction* and *non-fiction* appropriately

TL14 to pose questions and record these in writing, prior to reading non-fiction to find answers;

TL15 to use a contents page and index to find way about text

TL16 to scan a text to find specific sections, e.g. key words or phrases, subheadings

TL17 to skim-read title, contents page, illustrations, chapter headings and sub-headings, to speculate what a book might be about

TL18 to evaluate the usefulness of a text for its purpose

TL19 to make simple notes from non-fiction texts, e.g. key words and phrases, page references, headings, to use in subsequent writing

TL20 to write non-fiction texts, using texts read as models for own writing, e.g. use of headings, sub-headings, captions

TL21 to write non-chronological reports based on structure of known texts

WL9 to learn new words from reading linked to particular topics, to build individual collections of personal interest or significant words

SL6 to turn statements into questions, learning a range of *wh* words typically used to open questions: *what, where, when, who* and to add question marks

SL7 to compare a variety of forms of questions from texts, e.g. asking for help, asking the time, asking someone to be quiet

Range:	Fiction and poetry: extended stories; stories by significant children's authors Non-fiction: information books including non-chronological reports
Texts:	*The Nation's Favourite Game* From *Soccer Star*, Michael Hardcastle
Resources:	Big Book 2C pp. 32–39 Pupil Book 2 pp. 52–53 Copymaster 11 or 22 Homework Book 2 p. 25

Preparation

- Day 2: you will need a non-fiction book about sport in order to display the cover.
- Days 4 and 5: it may be useful to have a selection of non-fiction texts about sport available for the children to refer to.

DAY 1

Big Book 2C pp. 32–33; Pupil Book 2 pp. 52–53

Shared reading

- Introduce the non-fiction extract on pages 32 to 33. How many children enjoy playing football? Read page 32.
- How many players make up a professional team? How long does a game usually last? How many children own a football strip of a favourite team? Give them an opportunity to describe the colours and emblems featured on their teams' strips. How do football boots differ from ordinary boots?
- Before you read page 33, ask the children to tell you what they think makes a good football player. Make a note of their responses. Read page 33. Discuss any of the aspects that the children had not thought of prior to reading this page.

Focused word/sentence work

- Look at how the word *football* is made up of two smaller words, which help reveal the meaning of the larger word.
- Note that a comma is needed after the word *shirt*, as more than two items are listed.
- Encourage the children to practise scanning the text to find a specific word or phrase. Who can find the words *soccer, goals, kit, energy* and *strikers* first? Discuss why scanning is a useful skill to develop.

Independent work

- The questions on page 53 of Pupil Book 2 test children's comprehension of the non-fiction extract they have been reading with you.

Plenary

- Re-read pages 32 and 33 together.

DAY 2

Big Book 2C pp. 34–36; Pupil Book 2 p. 53

Shared reading

- Introduce the fiction extract from *Soccer Star*, which begins on page 34. Remind the children of the difference between factual writing (such as the extract they read on Day 1) and fiction.
- Read pages 34 and 35. Talk about Oscar's nick-name, "Oz". How many children in your class like to be called by a shortened version of their own names? What is Oscar's fantastic news?
- Read page 36. What does Oscar mean by "real" boots? Can the children remember a time when they were too excited to sleep? What were they excited about?

Focused word/sentence work

- Show the children a front cover of a non-fiction book about sport. Ask them to think about what the chapter headings of such a book might be. Write a list of their suggestions. How many different sports are the children able to think of? What other information might be included in a non-fiction book about sport, e.g. famous sports personalities, keeping fit, sporting awards?
- Read through the chapter headings on the contents page of your book about sport. Did the children guess any of the titles correctly?

Independent work

- The exercise on page 53 of Pupil Book 2 poses questions about a contents page from a book about sport.

Plenary

- Look again at your book about sport. Draw the children's attention to the different features of a non-fiction text: contents title, page, illustrations, chapter headings, sub-headings, captions, index, and glossary.

DAY 3

Big Book 2C pp. 37–39; Pupil Book 2 p. 53

Shared reading

- Ask the children to re-tell the story *Soccer Star* so far. Why was Oscar unable to sleep? Read pages 37 to 39. What do the children think about the way this extract ends? Do they think Mum is right to insist that Oscar goes to his grandparents' wedding anniversary?
- Explain that this extract has been taken from an extended story. Ask the children to predict how the story ends.

Focused word/sentence work

- How often does an anniversary occur? What other special events do people celebrate annually?
- Discuss the use of italics for emphasis on page 39: *"first", "can't", "know"*. Practise reading the sentences containing these words appropriately.
- Look at the questions in the text on pages 37 to 39: "What on earth are you up to?", "Who said you could wear your new boots in bed?", "When is the big match?", "What's a wedding anniver-whatever-you-said?". Write these questions on the board and underline the opening words. Can the children think of any other words typically used to begin a question, e.g. *How, Why, Where*? Ask them to think of other questions beginning with these words.

Independent work

- Children who complete exercises A and B on page 53 of Pupil Book 2 could write a few questions about different sports, using the words you discussed together during the word work session. They may use non-fiction texts at a later date to find answers to their questions.

Plenary

- Give the children a variety of statements and ask them to turn them into questions orally, e.g. *My name is. . . (What is your name?); My favourite film star is. . . (Who is your favourite film star?); I live in. . . (Where do you live?).*

DAY 4

Pupil Book 2 p. 53

Shared writing

- Discuss the writing challenge on page 53 of Pupil Book 2. Find out from the children which sports they want to write about (re-read the list of sports on the contents page together). Decide upon one of these sports to write about collectively.
- Decide upon a couple of sub-headings. What information will need to be included in the main text? Make notes. Talk about any pictures the children would like to include and possible captions to go with them.

Focused word/sentence work

- Using your notes of the children's ideas, help the children construct sentences to produce a non-chronological report about the chosen sport.

Independent work

- The children may begin planning their own page of factual information about their chosen sports, either independently or in pairs. Remind them that they will need a main heading, possibly a sub-heading or two and one or two pictures with captions. The information may extend to several pages, depending on the ability of the children and how much extra time is available outside the literacy hour.

Plenary

- Review some of the children's work and discuss ways of developing and improving it.
- Take a survey of the different types of sport the children have chosen to write about.

DAY 5

Big Book 2C pp. 32–39

Shared reading

- Re-read the non-fiction extract on pages 32 and 33.

Focused word/sentence work

- Formulate questions relating to the text, e.g. "How long does a game of football usually last for?" "How many players make up a professional team?" "What special clothes do football players wear?"

Independent work

- The children may continue working on their non-fiction writing about a chosen sport. Once all the children have completed their writing and presented it effectively, the work may be compiled to make a class "Book of Sport". The children could help produce a contents page, glossary and index.

Plenary

- Re-read the extract from *Soccer Star* on pages 34-39.

Consolidation and extension

- Read the complete version of Michael Hardcastle's extended story, *Soccer Star*, to see if Oscar gets to play for his school team.
- Use Copymaster 11 or 22 to produce a passport for, or write a character profile of, Oscar.
- Ask the children to write questions about different sports which may then be researched using non-fiction texts.

Homework

- Page 26 of Homework Book 2 is a wordsearch puzzle on the topic of sport. Point out that the words may be found by reading across or down the page. You may like to provide less able children with a word list of the words they are looking for: "basketball", "cycling", "football", "hockey","netball", "running","swimming", "tennis".

Unit 26

Fangs

Key Learning Objectives

TL3 to notice the difference between spoken and written forms through re-telling known stories, comparing oral versions with the written text

TL10 to write sustained stories, using their knowledge of story elements: narrative, settings, characterisation, dialogue and the language of story

WL10 to use synonyms and other alternative words/phrases that express same or similar meanings; to collect and discuss similarities and shades of meaning to extend and enhance writing

SL3 to use standard forms of verbs in speaking and writing, e.g. *catch/caught, see/saw, go/went* and to use the past tense consistently for narration

Range:	Fiction: extended stories
Texts:	From *Fangs*, Malorie Blackman
Resources:	Big Book 2C pp. 40–46 Pupil Book 2 pp. 54–55 Homework Book page 27

DAY 1

Big Book 2C pp. 40–41; Pupil Book 2 pp. 54–55

Shared reading

- Introduce the fiction extract from *Fangs* by Malorie Blackman. Read pages 40 and 41.
- Do the children think that the boy will go into the pet shop and buy the spider? Look at the illustration. What sort of spider is it? What does the spider dislike about living in a pet shop?
- Who is telling this story?

Focused word/sentence work

- What words does the author use to describe the boy's smile (*genuine, friendly, admiring*)? What words describe the spider's grin (*biggest, cheesiest, fangiest*)? Compare the words *smiled, beamed* and *grin.* Ask the children to think about why the author has used three different words to describe the same action.
- Look for other details and descriptions that the author has used to make the writing more interesting, e.g. "*serious* face", "he tapped again *very gently*".

Independent work

- Ask the children to complete the comprehension exercise on page 55 of the Pupil Book 2.

Plenary

- Ask the class to re-tell the extract they read at the beginning of the literacy hour in their own words. Re-read pages 40 and 41 and discuss the differences between the spoken and written forms.

DAY 2

Big Book 2C pp. 42–44; Pupil Book 2 p. 55

Shared reading

- Read pages 42 to 44.
- How did Mrs Bucket describe the tarantula? Had she had a lot of offers for the spider?
- How much did the tarantula cost? How much money did Nathan have?
- What was the spider's name?

Focused word/sentence work

- Focus on words which show that this story is written in the past tense, e.g. *mouthed, ran, worked*. The children should be familiar with the *-ed* ending but may need more help with other forms, e.g. *ran*. Remind them of the work they did on past tense in Unit 22. Are the children able to tell you what these words would be if the story was being told in the present tense?

Independent work

- The exercises on page 55 of Pupil Book 2 provide further practise of writing verbs in the past tense.

Plenary

- Write a few verbs on the board in the present tense, e.g. *see, go, eat, write*. Ask volunteers to tell you what each word would be if we were writing about something that had happened in the past. Invite them to write the new word on the board.
- Re-enact the scene that took place in the pet shop between Mrs Bucket and Nathan.

DAY 3

Big Book 2C pp. 44–46; Pupil Book 2 p. 55

Shared reading

- Re-read the second half of page 44 before reading pages 45 and 46.
- Talk about the way the extract ends. What do the children think will happen next? Will Fangella be sorry that Nathan bought her? What will Nathan's Mum say? Will she allow Nathan to keep the tarantula?

Focused word/sentence work

- Remind the children of the work they did on synonyms (words and phrases that have the same or similar meaning) in Unit 22. Revise this work, asking the children to think of alternative words to some of those that arose in today's extract, e.g. *scooped, pondered, glanced, groaned*.
- Re-read from "'Hi, I'm Nathan,' the boy said" . . . to "'You're going to love it at my house, Fangs,' puffed Nathan" at the top of page 46. Focus on all the words that the author has used instead of *said*: *told, pondered, repeated, wondered, groaned, puffed*. Look at how each of these words gives a little more information than the word "said". Talk about the extra richness that the variety of words used by the author gives the text.

Can the children think of other words that could be used in place of *said* in their own writing, e.g. *whispered, shouted, asked, begged, demanded*?

Independent work

- For children who complete exercise A on page 55 of Pupil Book 2, exercise B provides further work on synonyms, based on the printed extract.

Plenary

- Discuss different ideas about what will happen next in the story of *Fangs*. Encourage the children to explore their ideas about what will happen between Nathan and his mother when he arrives home with the spider through role-play.

DAY 4

Big Book 2C p. 46; Pupil Book 2 p. 55

- Remind the children of the ideas they came up with during the plenary session of Day 4. Read through the writing task on page 55 of Pupil Book 2.
- Re-read page 46 to remind the children of the point from which they will continue the story. Establish that the story will be continued by the spider (in the first person), which will mean using the personal pronoun *I*.
- Note down the children's ideas for what will happen next in the story, perhaps by beginning with the spider's response to Nathan's alarming words. Help the children to produce a piece of cohesive narrative.

Focused word/sentence work

- Re-read page 46 of Big Book 2C before reading through the writing you have produced with the children, making sure that they are happy with the content. Look for opportunities to improve the writing, e.g. repeated or uninteresting words which could be replaced.
- Check for grammatical agreement between verbs and nouns/pronouns. Make sure that there is consistent use of past tense verbs. Where there is inconsistency in verb tense, see if the children are able to tell you what is wrong and correct as necessary.
- Check the punctuation together.

Independent work

- The children should now be well prepared for continuing the story of *Fangs* in their own way. You may like to re-read page 46 of Big Book 2C one more time to remind the children of the point from which they are to take up the story.

Plenary

- Invite a few of the children to read their story continuation to the rest of the class. Draw attention to the best features of each and check for consistency of tense. Make sure that the children have all continued the story in the first person, as though Fangella is narrating.

DAY 5

Big Book 2C pp. 40–46

Shared reading

- Read the entire extract from *Fangs* together, without interruption.

Focused word/sentence work

- Discuss and evaluate the story extract as a whole. Which words and phrases do the children think are particularly funny, interesting or effective? Encourage the children to give reasons for their preferences.

Independent work

- The children may use this time to complete the story writing they began on Day 4.

Plenary

- Choose different children to read aloud their story endings. Discuss with the rest of the class any ideas they came up with which differ from those they have heard.

Consolidation and extension

- Read the entire version of Malorie Blackman's extended story, *Fangs*, to find out what happens when Nathan takes Fangella home.
- Use non-fiction books to find out factual information about tarantulas. Make notes and present the information appropriately, using texts read as models for own writing.

Homework

- Page 27 of Homework Book 2 is a letter-writing activity which requires children to think of a list of reasons why Nathan should be allowed to keep his pet tarantula.

Unit 27 Playing With Words

Key Learning Objectives

TL6 to read, respond imaginatively, recommend and collect examples of humorous poems

TL8 to discuss meanings of words and phrases that create humour, and sound effects in poetry, e.g. nonsense poems, tongue-twisters, riddles, and to classify poems into simple types; to make class anthologies

TL11 to use humorous verse as a structure for children to write their own by adaptation, mimicry or substitution; to invent own riddles, language puzzles, jokes, nonsense sentences etc., derived from reading; to write tongue-twisters or alliterative sentences; to select words with care, re-reading and listening to their effect

WL2 to reinforce work on discriminating syllables in reading and spelling from previous term

WL3 to discriminate, spell and read the phoneme *ea* (as in *head*)

Range:	Poetry: texts with language play, e.g. riddles, tongue-twisters, humorous verse and stories
Texts:	From *Laughter is an Egg*, John Agard From *Riddles and Rhymes and Rigmaroles*, John Cunliffe *Betty Botter . . .*, Traditional
Resources:	Big Book 2C pp. 47–49 Pupil Book 2 pp. 56–57 Copymaster 24 Homework Book 2 p. 28

Preparation

- Day 1: make a set of word cards featuring objects or creatures, e.g. *cow, plane, television, jelly, elephant, dragon.*
- Day 2: the children will need hand mirrors, such as those used for symmetry work in mathematics.

DAY 1

Big Book 2C pp. 47–48; Pupil Book 2 pp. 56–57

Shared reading

- Introduce the riddles on pages 47 and 48. Can anyone tell you what a riddle is? Explain that it is a puzzle to be solved, often told in rhyme.
- Read the first riddle by John Cunliffe on page 47. What is it about? Can the children explain the line "Where right is left and left is right"?
- Read the second riddle by John Cunliffe on page 47. What is it about? What is the "something" it tells? Have the children heard the saying "time flies"? Can they explain what it means?
- Read *Hatch Me a Riddle* by John Agard on page 48. What is it about? What is the "yellow moon"? Can the children find a clue to the riddle in the title ("*Hatch* me a Riddle")?

Focused word/sentence work

- Find the rhyming words in John Cunliffe's riddles (*hand/land; right/night; see/be; tell/well; word/bird*).
- Look at the word "steady". Can the children tell you the sound of the third phoneme, *ea*? Remind the children of the work they did on this spelling pattern in Unit 24. Can they remember any other words containing *ea* as in *steady* e.g. *bread, dreadful, head, ready*? Invite volunteers to try spelling the words that are suggested on the board.

Independent work

- Ask the children to answer the questions about the riddles they have read today on page 57 of Pupil Book 2.

Plenary

- Play "Give Us a Clue". Give a volunteer a card with the word of an object or creature on (see **Preparation**) and ask them to give the class one clue at a time about it, e.g. *it eats grass; it has four legs, it gives us milk.* In between clues, the rest of the class may make guesses as to what it is. The first child to guess correctly takes the next go at giving clues.

DAY 2

Big Book 2C pp. 47–48; Pupil Book 2 p. 57

Shared reading

- Re-read the riddles on pages 47 and 48.
- Can the children explain the line "once open, for ever open" in John Agard's riddle?
- Which of these riddles do the children like best? Ask them to give reasons for their preferences.

Focused word/sentence work

- Can the children spot which of the lines in John Agard's riddle are repeated?
- Find all the words in John Agard's riddle that contain *oo*. Which word is the odd one out with the *oo* phoneme making a different sound from the others (*door*)?

Independent work

- The children will need hand mirrors to read answers to the jokes on page 57 of Pupil Book 2. Explain that jokes are a little like riddles in that they are puzzles to be solved, but they should also be funny.

Plenary

- Read through the jokes in section A on page 57 of Pupil Book 2. Which of these jokes did the children find the funniest? Discuss what is humorous about each, checking that the children have understood the play on words.

DAY 3

Big Book 2C p. 49; Pupil Book 2 p. 57

Shared reading

- Introduce the tongue-twister on page 49. Who can tell you what a tongue-twister is? Before you read the tongue-twister, find out if the children know what "batter" is, what is it made of and what is it used to make?
- Read through the tongue-twister slowly together.

Focused word/sentence work

- Talk about what it is that makes a tongue-twister humorous.
- How many words can the children find that contain the letters *b* and *t*. Point out that many of these words are repeated several times.
- Can the children find words with one syllable? Two syllables? More than two syllables? Point out that in every four lines there are 16 syllables. Recite the rhyme, clapping the syllables in groups of four. Note the very regular rhythm of this tongue-twister.

Independent work

- Exercise B on page 57 of Pupil Book 2 requires the children to match joke questions to their correct answers.

Plenary

- Look at the jokes in section B together. What is funny about each? Which joke do the children think is the funniest?
- Find out if the children know any other tongue-twisters, e.g. "Peter Piper", "She Sells Sea Shells". Learn and recite them together.

DAY 4

Pupil Book 2 p. 57; Copymaster 24

Shared writing

- Choose one of the ideas on page 57 of Pupil Book 2 to write a riddle about together, e.g. *a pair of glasses*. Ask the children to think of as many different ideas as possible about the item you have chosen, e.g.
  I have two windows.
  I have frames but no pictures.
  You need two ears and a nose to wear me.
  Without me I am difficult to find.

  The sentences need not necessarily be written in the first person.

Focused word/sentence work

- Once you have a reasonable list of clues, decide which lines to keep and which to cut. Cut lines which are either too complicated or will give away the answer too quickly.
- Decide the best order in which to put your sentences. Perhaps save the clues which are most likely to give away the answer until last.

Independent work

- Copymaster 24 depicts a pair of glasses, an aeroplane and a chair. There is room next to each picture for children to make up a riddle. There is also a space for them to write another "mystery" riddle.

Plenary

- Invite children to read aloud any riddles they are particularly pleased with. Encourage the rest of the class to respond by saying which lines they think work best and why.

DAY 5

Big Book 2C p. 49

Shared reading

- Practise reading this tongue-twister as quickly and clearly as possible. You may like to divide the class up to read different sections in turn.

Focused word/sentence work

- Make up a few alliterative tongue-twisters of your own. Give the children a few ideas to get them started, e.g.
  Thomas Taylor took a taxi to . . .
  Wendy Wendon wore wellies wherever she went . . .
  My mum moans when I make a mess . . .

Independent work

- Allow time for the children to finish writing their own riddles.

Plenary

- Choose different children to read out their completed riddles.

Consolidation and extension

- Ask the children to collect other tongue-twisters and riddles to make class anthologies. Encourage them to recommend their favourites to the rest of the class, saying what it is that they like about a particular poem.

Homework

- Page 28 of Homework Book 2 offers children the chance to write some tongue-twisters of their own. Suggest that they use a dictionary to find words beginning with the same letters.

Unit 28 Bothersome Brothers

Key Learning Objectives

TL6	to read, respond imaginatively, recommend and collect examples of humorous stories, extracts, poems
TL7	to compare books by different authors on similar themes; to evaluate giving reasons
TL8	to discuss meanings of words and phrases that create humour, and sound effects in poetry, e.g. nonsense poems, tongue-twisters, riddles, and to classify poems into simple types; to make class anthologies
TL11	to use humorous verse as a structure for children to write their own by adaptation, mimicry or substitution; to invent own riddles, language puzzles, jokes, nonsense sentences etc., derived from reading; to write tongue-twisters or alliterative sentences; to select words with care, re-reading and listening to their effect
WL10	to use synonyms and other alternative words/phrases that express same or similar meanings; to collect and discuss similarities and shades of meaning to extend and enhance writing
SL2	to learn the need for grammatical agreement, matching verbs to nouns/pronouns, e.g. *I am; the children are;* to use simple gender forms, e.g. *his/her* correctly.

Range:	Fiction and poetry: extended stories; stories by significant children's authors; texts with language play, e.g. tongue-twisters, humorous verse
Texts:	*Brother*, Mary Ann Hoberman From *Press Play*, Anne Fine
Resources:	Big Book 2C pp. 50–56 Pupil Book 2 pp. 58–59 Homework Book 2 p. 29

DAY 1

Big Book 2C p. 50; Pupil Book 2 pp. 58–59

Shared reading

- Read the poem by Mary Ann Hoberman on page 50 of Big Book 2C. What sort of poem is it?
- Why did the girl take her little brother to her mother? What did her mother reply? What did the girl's father tell her? What did she do with her "little bother of a brother" in the end?

Focused word/sentence work

- How many words ending in *-er* can the children find? Remind the children of the work they did on this phoneme last term. Can they think of any other words ending in *-er*?
- Which words are repeated throughout the poem (*little, brother, bother, said*)? Explain that the poet has deliberately repeated words for effect. Do the children like the way this has been done? If the author was writing a story, she would probably want to avoid overuse of these words. What similar words can the children think of that could be used in place of *little, bother, said*? What word did "the Great One" use to describe her little brother in the story by Judy Blume (Unit 3)?

Independent work

- The questions on page 59 of Pupil Book 2 relate to the poem.

Plenary

- Practise reading the poem by Mary Ann Hoberman.

DAY 2

Big Book 2C pp. 51-53; Pupil Book 2 p. 59

Shared reading

- Introduce the extract from *Press Play* by Anne Fine. What do the children think the title means?
- Read pages 51 and 52. Check that all the children have understood what is happening. Why had Mum prepared a tape of instructions for her children? Where was she? Where was Dad?
- Read page 53. Why did Tasha not want to feed her little brother? What did Mum mean when she said "carry me down carefully to the kitchen"?

Focused word/sentence work

- What do the children notice about the way Mum's speech is printed (in italics)?
- Look at the contractions *we'll, you'll, I'll*. Explain that in everyday speech we tend to "squash" words together in this way. Can the children tell you which words have been put together in these examples (*we will; you will; I will*)?

Independent work

- The exercises on page 59 of Pupil Book 2 revise work on synonyms.

Plenary

- Re-read pages 51 to 53.

DAY 3

Big Book 2C pp. 54–56; Pupil Book 2 p. 59

Shared reading

- Recap briefly on the story so far before reading pages 54 to 56.

Focused word/sentence work

- Look for examples of simple gender forms, e.g. "Tasha opened and closed *her* mouth like an actor"; "Tasha looked down at *her* thin cotton cowboy shirt"; "*he* stuck out *his* bottom lip, ready to cry"; etc. In each case, can the children tell you who *her, he, his* etc. is referring to?

Independent work

- Children who complete the exercises on page 59 of Pupil Book 2 could write sentences using the words *his*, *her* and *their*.

Plenary

- Read through the passage (Exercise B) together and find out what words the children have thought of to replace the words in bold type.

DAY 4

Big Book 2C p. 50; Pupil Book 2 pp. 58–59

Shared writing

- Re-read *Brother* by Mary Ann Hoberman on page 50 of Big Book 2C.
- Look at the different suggestions on page 59 of Pupil Book 2 for the subject of a humorous poem about a fictional family member. Choose one to write about together.
- Discuss what it is that makes Mary Ann Hoberman's poem amusing. Which elements would the children like to imitate, e.g. alliteration, repetition?
- Make a note of all the children's suggestions for the poem, without worrying too much at this stage about the organisation of their ideas.

Focused word/sentence work

- Discuss all the ideas you have noted down. Which do the children think work most successfully? Decide together how best to arrange the ideas to form a poem. Do not focus unduly on rhyme unless it arises naturally in the poem, as this may distract the children from selecting the best vocabulary.

Independent work

- Give the children a chance to write their own humorous poems using one of the ideas from page 59 of Pupil Book 2.

Plenary

- Listen to some of the children's poems so far. Use this time to think of ways to improve and develop their work in order to raise the quality of poetry that is produced on Day 5.

DAY 5

Big Book 2C pp. 51–56

Shared reading

- Re-read the extract from *Press Play* in its entirety.

Focused word/sentence work

- Explain that the extract is only the beginning of the story. What other instructions do the children think will be on the tape recorder to assist Nicky and Tasha in getting Little Joe ready for nursery and themselves ready for school? Write a list of the instructions that the class give and discuss the order in which they should appear.

Independent work

- The children may use this time to complete their humorous poems.

Plenary

- Choose different children to read their completed poems to the rest of the class. Invite the class to comment on what they like best about each young poet's work.

Consolidation and extension

- Read the entire extended story *Press Play* by Anne Fine.
- Re-read the extract from *A Worm's Eye View* by Jan Mark (Unit 8, Big Book 2A). Discuss the similarities and differences between the two extracts which share a similar theme: looking after a troublesome younger brother or cousin. Can the children find other stories which share this theme?
- Encourage the children to collect their favourite humorous poems for a class anthology. Ask them to recommend their favourites to the rest of the class, saying what it is that they like most about a particular poem.

Homework

- Page 29 in Homework Book 2 provides practice in using simple gender forms.

Unit 29 Communication

Key Learning Objectives

TL13 to understand the distinction between fact and fiction; to use the terms *fact*, *fiction* and *non-fiction* appropriately

TL15 to use a contents page and index to find way about text

TL16 to scan a text to find specific sections, e.g. key words or phrases, subheadings

TL20 to write non-fiction texts, using texts read as models for own writing, e.g. use of headings, sub-headings, captions

TL21 to write non-chronological reports based on structure of known texts

WL2 to reinforce work on discriminating syllables in reading and spelling from previous term

WL9 to learn new words from reading linked to particular topics, to build individual collections of personal interest or significant words

SL4 to use commas in lists

Range:	Non-fiction: information books including non-chronological reports
Texts:	*How do we Communicate?* *Helen Keller*
Resources:	Big Book 2C pp. 57–60 Pupil Book 2 pp. 60–61 Copymaster 25 Homework Book 2 p. 30

Preparation

- Days 4 and 5: have available a range of appropriate non-fiction texts and dictionaries for children to use, as a model for their non-chronological reports, and to find out more about different types of domestic machinery.

DAY 1

Big Book 2C pp. 57–58; Pupil Book 2 pp. 60–61

Shared reading

- Before you begin reading, establish what the children understand "communication" to mean.
- Read the introduction on page 57 of Big Book 2C. Ask the children to give examples of ways of communicating with words, sounds, movement and pictures.
- Read to the end of page 58. Which machines bring words and music to us? Which enables us to speak to people many miles away? What are fax machines used for? How many ways can a computer be used to help us communicate? Explain "e-mail" and the "Internet".

Focused word/sentence work

- Write the words *television* and *telephone* on the board and underline *tele*. Can the children think of any other words that begin in this way, e.g. *telescope*, *telegram*? What do these words have in common?
- How many syllables can the children hear in the words *communicate*, *information*, *radio*, *television* and *computer*? Who can find each of these words first by scanning the text?

Independent work

- The children may now answer the questions (which you have discussed orally) on page 61 of Pupil Book 2.

Plenary

- Can the children think of ways of communicating without using machines or speech, e.g. newspapers, books, letter writing, morse code, smoke signals, sign language, braille? Who uses/used these forms of communication?

DAY 2

Big Book 2C pp. 57–58; Pupil Book 2 p. 61

Shared reading

- Re-read pages 57 and 58. Look at the sentences about each type of machine. Would it matter if they were presented in a different order? Why not? What is the main heading (*Communication*)? Can the children find a sub-heading (*How do we Communicate?*)? Can they think of another sub-heading which could be used in place of the statement (*We often use machines to communicate*)?
- Is the writing on pages 57 and 58 fact or fiction? Can the children explain the different meanings of these two terms? Can they think of examples of fiction? Keep all definitions as simple as possible. The distinction between *fact* and *opinion* will be made in Key Stage Two.

Focused word/sentence work

- Write on the board: *We can communicate with words, sounds, movement and pictures.* Explain that where more than two things are listed, it is helpful to use commas. Point out that a comma is not necessary before the word *and* (although they may sometimes see it used). Practise using the comma in a number of different lists, e.g. machines used in the kitchen. Once the children have offered words for each particular list, invite volunteers to put the commas in the appropriate places.

Independent work

- The exercises on page 61 of Pupil Book 2 reinforce the distinction between fact and fiction.

Plenary

- Write a few more lists for the children to practise adding commas in the appropriate places.

DAY 3

Big Book 2C pp. 59–60; Pupil Book 2 p. 61

Shared reading

- Find out if any of the children have heard of Helen Keller. Read pages 59 and 60. What made Helen's mother realise that she was blind? How did she discover that Helen was also deaf?
- Why did Helen behave badly as a small child?
- Why would it be especially difficult for Helen to learn to talk? What other skills did she learn?

- What is "Braille"?
- What would the children miss most about being unable to see? What sounds would they miss most if they were unable to hear?

Focused word/sentence work

- If the children were alive at the same time as Helen Keller, what questions would they like to have asked her? Make a list of these questions and spend time thinking about the answers she may have given to each.

Independent work

- Children who complete the exercises on page 61 within the given time may like to draw a picture of what they would miss most if they were unable to see. Ask them to write a caption to go with their picture.

Plenary

- Ask the children who had time to draw pictures and write captions to share them with the rest of the class. Give children who did not have time to produce a drawing the opportunity to talk about what they would miss most if they could not see.
- Do the children know anyone who is deaf or blind? What do they like most about that person? How does that person cope with his or her disability?

DAY 4

Pupil Book 2 p. 61; Copymaster 25

Shared writing

- Read the writing task on page 61 of Pupil Book 2. Think about machines we use in our kitchens. Write a list of all the machines the pupils can think of, e.g. *cooker, washing machine, microwave, fridge, kettle*. You may wish to include non-electrical items, such as a can-opener.
- What will the main heading be? Decide whether you want to group any of the items that the children have listed under a sub-heading, e.g. *Machines that help us to cook*. Which items do the children think should be illustrated? Where will the pictures go? Write captions to explain the function of each item.

Focused word/sentence work

- Discuss the way the information has been organised. Are the children happy with the way their ideas have been presented? Encourage them to tell you what they will be keeping the same in their own work and what they would like to change.
- If there are lists of more than two items, ask the children to check that the commas are in the right places.

Independent work

- The children may now begin their own information pages, either alone or in pairs. You may like them to plan their pages before producing their final pieces of non-chronological writing. Copymaster 25 will provide less able children with additional support to help them complete this activity.
- Encourage all the children to use appropriate non-fiction texts and dictionaries to find out more about different types of household machines. Direct them towards the contents pages and indexes to check the suitability of the non-fiction texts for the task in hand and locate specific information. Remind them that dictionaries can provide them with definitions of particular machines which will help them when writing captions.

Plenary

- Ask the children to swap their work with a friend. Ask them to comment on what they like best about each other's work and give suggestions for possible improvements. Invite children to tell the rest of the class about any useful comments their partner/friends made. Do the others agree?

DAY 5

Big Book 2C pp. 59–60

Shared reading

- Re-read pages 59 and 60.
- How do the children think Annie Sullivan taught Helen to spell words like "doll"?

Focused word/sentence work

- Ask the children to practise spelling a word into their partner's hand using a finger to "write" the letters. Begin with the word *doll*. Write three simple words on the board. Ask the children to choose one word, without saying it aloud, and spell it into their partner's hand. Can the partners guess which of the three words it was?

Independent work

- The children may use this time to complete their non-fiction texts.

Plenary

- Spend some time looking at the children's finished work. Many will need time outside the literacy hour to complete the task and compile simple books using their pages of non-fiction writing.
- Think of ways that we can help deaf people. Remind children that many deaf people lip-read and need to see our faces when we speak in order to do this. Explain that we should not shout as this distorts our mouths and makes it difficult for a lip-reader to understand us. Ask the children to try speaking without sound for a partner to try to lip-read what is being said.

Consolidation and extension

- Read a more detailed account of the life of Helen Keller. Find out about the Frenchman, Louis Braille and the origins of Braille, used by many blind and partially sighted people throughout the world today.
- If possible, bring in a piece of writing in braille for the children to see and touch.

Homework

- Page 30 of Homework Book 2 provides further practice in using commas in lists.

Unit 30

Little Red Riding Hood and the Wolf

Key Learning Objectives

TL3	to notice the difference between spoken and written forms through re-telling known stories: compare oral versions with the written text
TL6	to read, respond imaginatively, recommend and collect examples of humorous stories, extracts, poems
TL7	to compare books by different authors on similar themes; to evaluate, giving reasons
TL8	to discuss meanings of words and phrases that create humour, and sound effects in poetry, e.g. nonsense poems, tongue-twisters, riddles, and to classify poems into simple types; to make class anthologies
TL10	to write sustained stories, using their knowledge of story elements: narrative, settings, characterisation, dialogue and the language of story
TL12	to write simple evaluations of books read and discussed giving reasons
WL3	to discriminate, spell and read the phoneme *ear* (as in *hear*)
WL10	to use synonyms and other alternative words/phrases that express same or similar meanings; to collect, discuss similarities and shades of meaning and use to extend and enhance writing

Range:	Fiction and poetry: stories by significant children's authors; texts with language play, e.g. riddles, tongue-twisters, humorous verse and stories
Texts:	From *Revolting Rhymes*, Roald Dahl
Resources:	Big Book 2C pp. 61–64 Pupil Book 2 pp. 62–63 Copymasters 22, 26 and 27 Assessment master, Term 3 Homework Book 2 p. 31

Preparation

- Day 2: you may find it useful to refer back to the story of *The Princess and the Pig* by Dick King-Smith in Big Book 2B, Unit 11.

DAY 1

Big Book 2C pp. 61–62; Pupil Book 2 pp. 62–63

Shared reading

- How many children have read a story or poem by Roald Dahl? Perhaps they have seen a film of one of his books? What can they tell you about Roald Dahl's stories and poems?
- Introduce "Little Red Riding Hood and the Wolf" from Roald Dahl's *Revolting Rhymes*. Read pages 61 and 62. Who is "the little girl in red"?
- What is different about the way Roald Dahl is telling this traditional story? Has he stuck to the original plot as the children remember it so far?

Focused word/sentence work

- Focus on the rhyming pairs that Roald Dahl has used. Turn the text away from the children and read through the rhyme, pausing for them to pre-empt the rhyming word at the end of every other line.
- What words has Roald Dahl used to describe the wolf's teeth? What word describes his grin? How many other words can the children think of that mean the same as *horrid*?

Independent work

- The comprehension questions on page 63 of Pupil Book 2 relate to the opening section of the extract *Little Red Riding Hood and the Wolf* by Roald Dahl.

Plenary

- Re-read pages 61 and 62 of Big Book 2C.

DAY 2

Big Book 2C pp. 63–64; Pupil Book 2 p. 63

Shared reading

- Remind the children of the point at which you left the extract on Day 1 before reading the conclusion on page 63. Do the children recognise the last line on the page, spoken by Little Red Riding Hood? What did she say in the original story?
- Read page 64 of Big Book 2C.
- Discuss what it is that the children find funny about this version of the famous story. What has Roald Dahl kept the same? What has he changed?

Focused word/sentence work

- Have any of the children tasted caviare? Ask them to describe the taste.
- Write *What great big ears you have* on the board and underline *ear*. Can the children recall any other words containing this phoneme? Invite them to help spell the words they suggest that contain *ear*.

Independent work

- Exercise A on page 63 of Pupil Book 2 focuses on the rhyming pairs used by Roald Dahl in the first half of *Little Red Riding Hood and the Wolf*.

Plenary

- Can the children remember another humorous re-telling of a famous story that they have read this year (*The Princess and the Pig* by Dick King-Smith)? Ask them to re-tell the story and compare it with Roald Dahl's *Little Red Riding Hood and the Wolf*. Which of the two stories do the children like best? Ask them to give reasons for their preferences.

DAY 3

Big Book 2C pp. 61–64; Pupil Book 2 p. 63; Copymaster 22

Shared reading

- Re-read the entire extract from *Revolting Rhymes* by Roald Dahl. What do the children think of the author's choice of title for the book that this tale is taken from? Is his version of the story more *revolting* than the original tale?

Focused word/sentence work

- Focus on the wide range of adjectives Roald Dahl has used. Which descriptions do the children think are the most effective?
- Challenge the children to think of other words which mean the same (in context) as *terrified, cried, big, small* (page 61); *eat, lovely* (page 63).

Independent work

- Exercise B on page 63 of Pupil Book 2 requires the children to draw the Wolf and write a few descriptive sentences about him. Some of the children may find this task easier using a copy of Copymaster 22.

Plenary

- Talk about the endings to the story of Little Red Riding Hood that the children are more familiar with (there may be a few variations). Can they think of any other, new ways to end the story?

DAY 4

Pupil Book 2 p. 63; Copymaster 26

Shared writing

- Talk about the writing challenge on page 63 of Pupil Book 2. Find out if the children would like to write a traditional ending to the story or another version of their own (request that they do not copy Roald Dahl's ending!). Help the class to write the story from the point at which Little Red Riding Hood enters the room. This will include the famous dialogue that takes place between herself and the Wolf.
- Remind the children of the ideas they thought of during the Plenary session on Day 3 when deciding how to end the shared writing.

Focused word/sentence work

- Focus on the choice of vocabulary, bearing in mind Roald Dahl's use of adjectives. Remind the children of the words he used in place of *said*, e.g. *cried, wailed, replied*.
- Are the children happy with the way that the story has been organised? Do they like the way the story ends (traditionally or otherwise)?
- Check through the punctuation of the writing together.

Independent work

- The children should now be well prepared for writing their own story ending using Copymaster 26.

Plenary

- Use this time to reflect on the texts that the children have read with you this year. Conduct a survey to find out the class's favourite story, poem and non-fiction writing. They may need a little reminding about the texts you have studied together. Encourage the children to give reasons for their preferences.

DAY 5

Big Book 2A, B or C; Copymaster 26 from Day 4; Copymaster 27

Shared reading

- Following the Plenary session on Day 4, select one of the children's favourite *Focus on Literacy* texts to re-read together. Discuss what it is that the children particularly enjoyed about this text.

Focused word/sentence work

- Reflect upon the objectives that have been met this year, finding out from the children aspects that they now feel more confident about, e.g. sentence punctuation, reading aloud. Remind the children of the areas you have been concentrating on particularly this term.
- Divide the class in half for a simple quiz, pulling together many of the teaching points you have been working on this year.

Independent work

- The children may use this time to complete the story writing they began on Day 4.

Plenary

- Model how to write a story evaluation. Use the sentence prompts given on Copymaster 27, relating them to the text that you shared during this session. The children may then write their own evaluation of a favourite text for homework or at some other appropriate time.

Consolidation and extension

- Use Copymaster 27 to write an evaluation of a book or story read this term, ideally the complete version of one of the *Focus on Literacy* extracts you have studied together.
- Read more of Roald Dahl's *Revolting Rhymes*. Make a collection of modern re-tellings of traditional tales.
- The Assessment master for Term 3 provides revision of teaching points covered this term as a means of assessing children's progress.

Homework

- Page 31 of Homework Book 2 takes a look at several of the different story characters the children have met this term.
- Page 32 of Homework Book 2 provides revision of some of the teaching points covered this year.

Copymasters

Name ______________________________

Look, Say, Cover, Write, Check

Look and say	Cover and write	Check ✓ ✗	Try again	Check ✓ ✗

Copymaster 2
Unit 1

Name ______________________

Something I Have Learned

Something which I found difficult to do was . . .

____

____

I needed to . . .

____

____

I was helped by . . .

____

____

In the end I . . .

____

____

I felt . . .

____

____

Copymaster 3
Unit 2

Name ______________________

New Shoes

Cut out the sentences along the dotted lines.
Put the sentences in the right order.

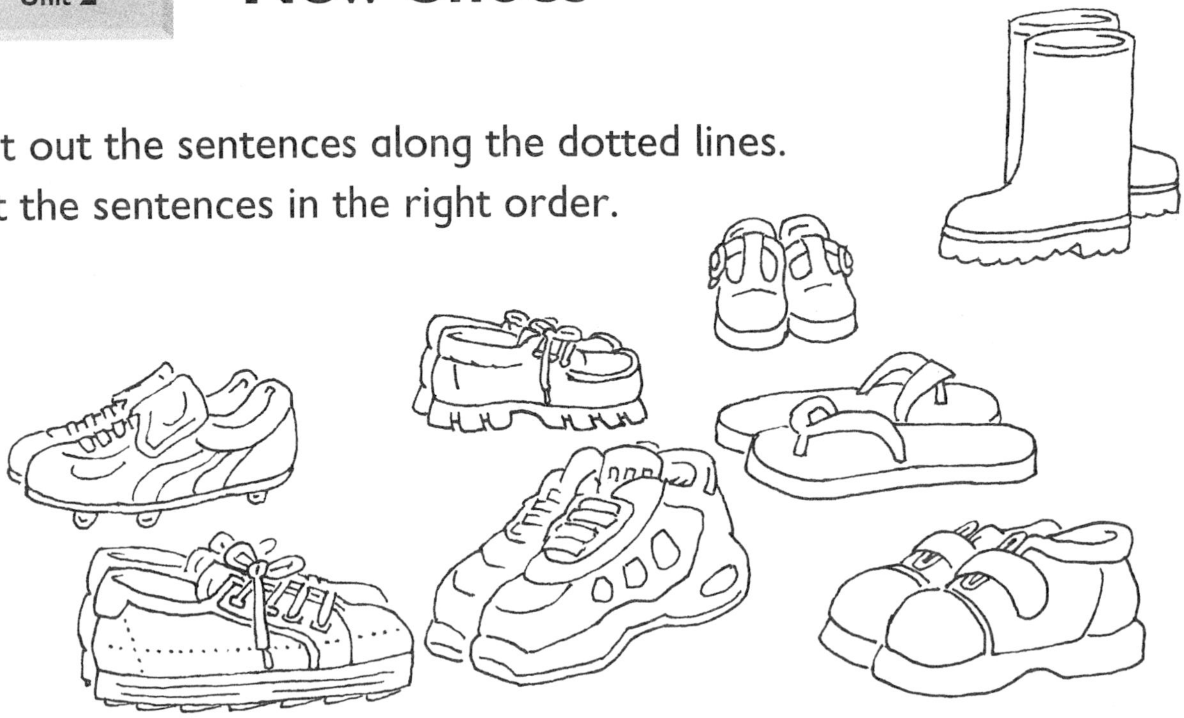

He chooses the pair that fits best.

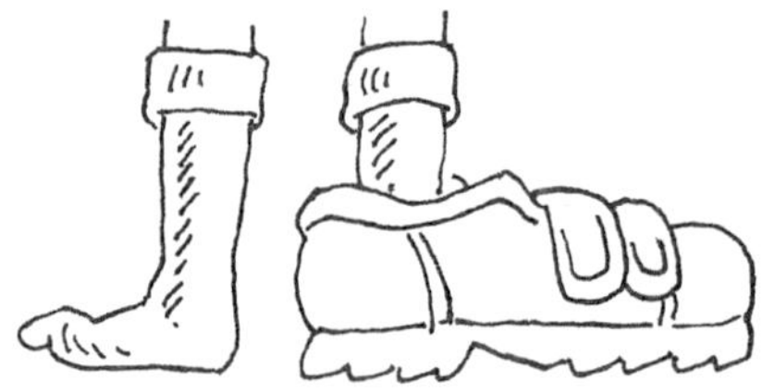

Then, Mr Berman goes to look for shoes in Peter's size.

Peter tries on two different pairs of shoes.

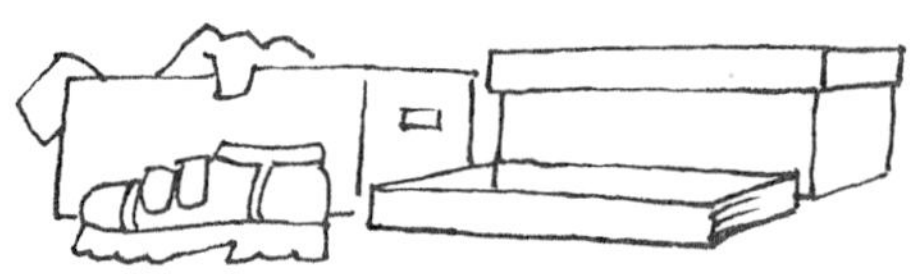

Finally, Mr Berman wraps the shoes for Peter to take home.

Peter has his feet measured.

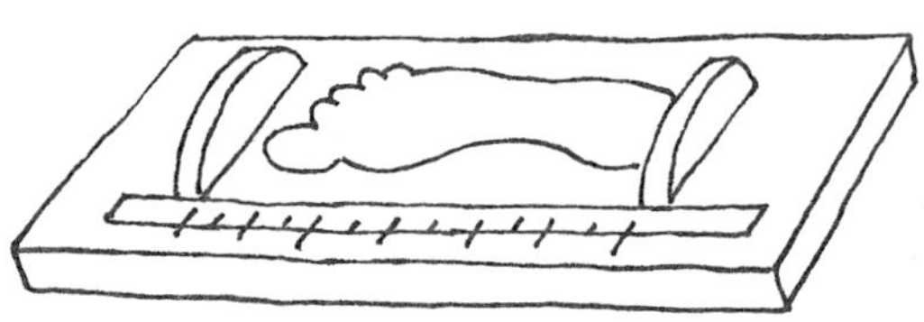

Copymaster 4
Unit 3

Name ______________________

How to Annoy Your Big Sister

1. Borrow her things without asking.

2. Put dinosaurs in her bed.

3. ______________________________

____

4. ______________________________

____

5. ______________________________

____

6. ______________________________

____

By the Pain

Copymaster 5
Unit 4

Name ______________________

Sorry Miss . . .

I have not done my homework because . . .

____

____

____

____

____

____

____

____

Name ____________________

My Special Day

On my special day I was celebrating . . .

____

____

Some of the people celebrating with me were . . .

____

____

I wore . . .

____

____

I felt . . .

____

____

The best part of the day was when . . .

____

____

____

____

Name ______________________

Instructions

Write instructions for cleaning out a hamster cage.
Don't forget to number your instructions.

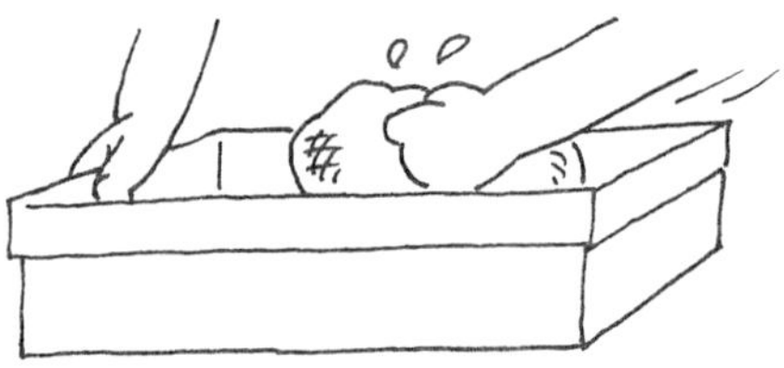

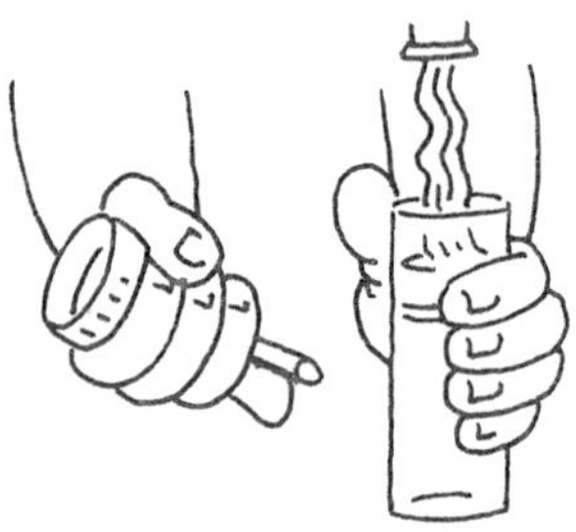

Copymaster 8
Unit 10

Name ______________________

Make Your Own Angel

You will need: template (Copymaster 9), scissors, coloured pens, glue, glitter, sequins.

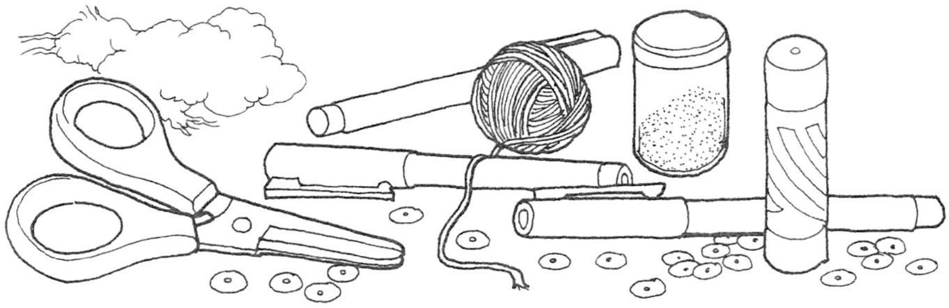

1. Cut out the template on Copymaster 9.

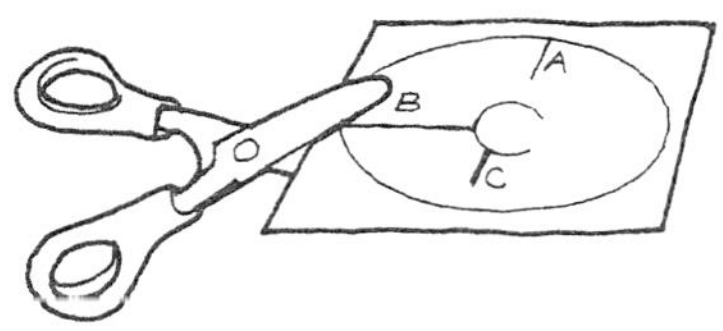

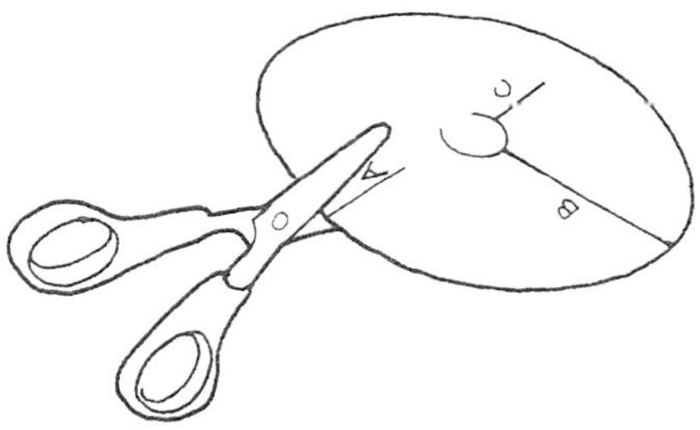

2. Carefully cut along line A.

3. Cut along lines B and C and the curved line in the middle of the circle.

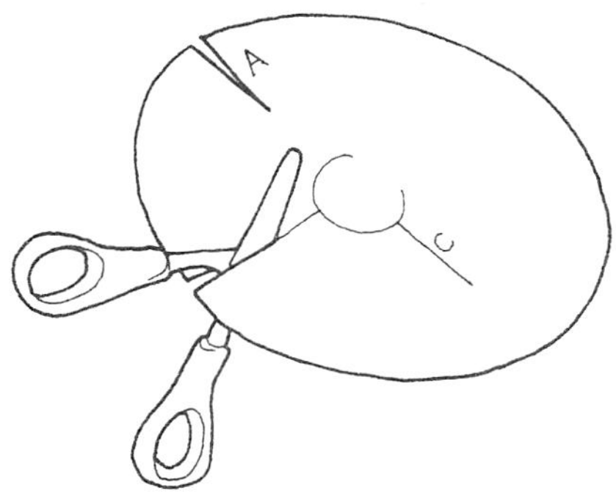

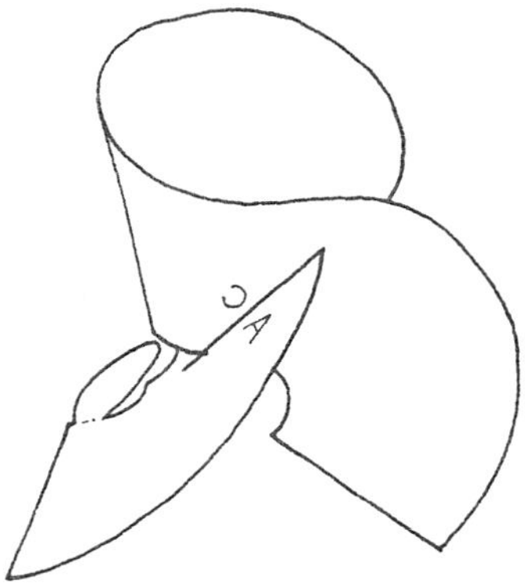

4. Fold the circle into a cone shape. Fit slot A over slot B.

5. Draw a face and stick on some hair.

6. Decorate the angel's robe and wings.

Copymaster 9
Unit 10

Name ______________________

Angel Template

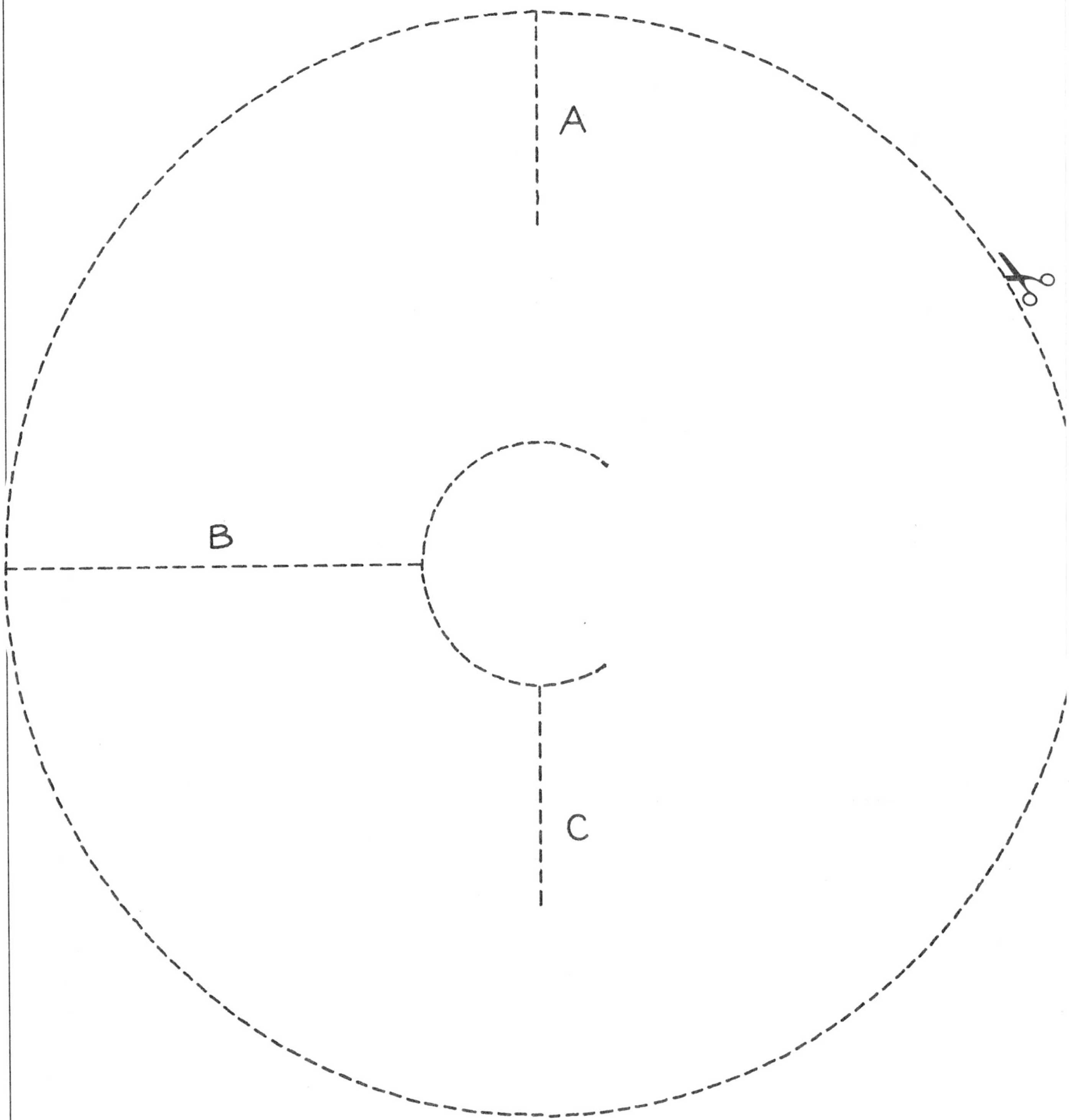

Name ______________________

Copymaster 10
Unit 11

The Frog Prince

Write what happens next . . .

Passport

Name

Character

Address

Date of Birth

Hobbies

Name

Copymaster 12
Unit 12

Name ____________

Glossary

Write a definition for each word.

boar ____________

piglet ____________

snout ____________

sow ____________

trotter ____________

Write a few sentences about pigs using some of these words.

Name ______________________

Dog, Cat and Monkey

Pretend you are Monkey.
Write about what you saw.

____

____

____

____

____

____

____

____

____

____

____

____

Name ______________________

My Favourite Food

I love ______________________

I can't get enough . . .

____

____

____

____

____

____

____

____

____

____

____

____

____

____

My Dictionary of Food

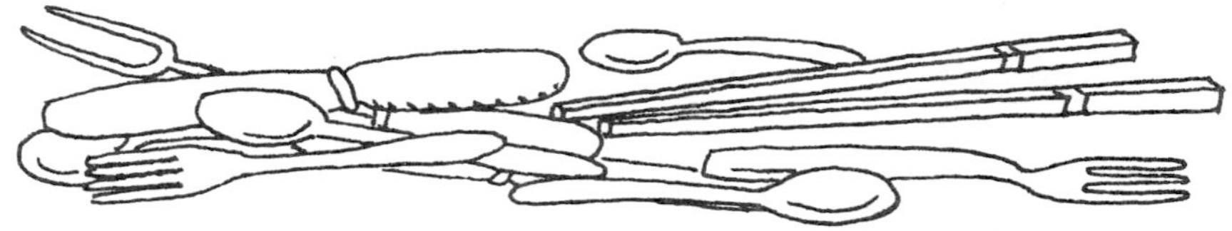

Name ______

Name of food	Description	Drawing

Name ____________________

Manji and the Raja

Write something the Raja said.

Describe the Raja.

____

____

____

____

Write something Manji said.

Describe Manji.

____

____

____

____

Copymaster 17
Unit 17

Name ______________________

ch as in "School"

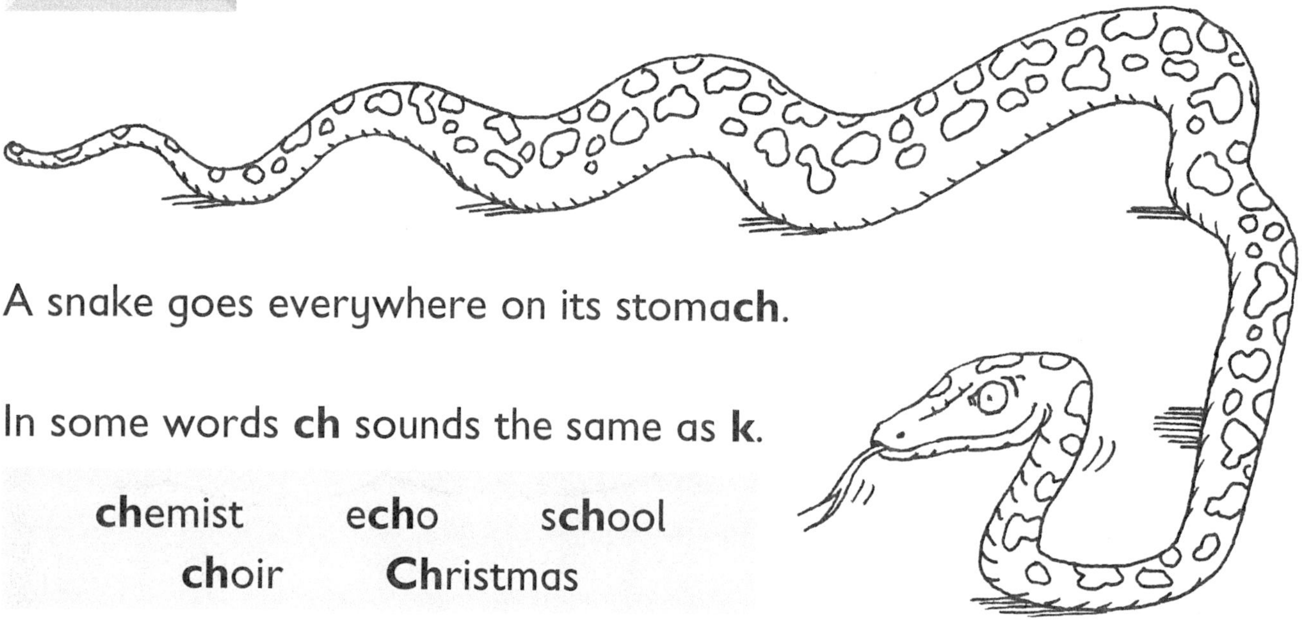

A snake goes everywhere on its stoma**ch**.

In some words **ch** sounds the same as **k**.

chemist　　e**ch**o　　s**ch**ool
choir　　**Ch**ristmas

Write the correct word in each space below.

The ________________ sells medicine.

My gran sings in the ________________.

There was an ________________ in the cave.

I hope it snows at ________________.

My sister likes going to ________________.

Underline **ch** when it sounds like **k** in the names below.

Christopher　　Charlie　　Michael　　Nicholas

Copymaster 18
Unit 18

Name ______________________

Snake Charm

Make a diagram to show how a snake sheds its skin.
Use words and pictures to explain what happens.

2. ______________________________
____
____

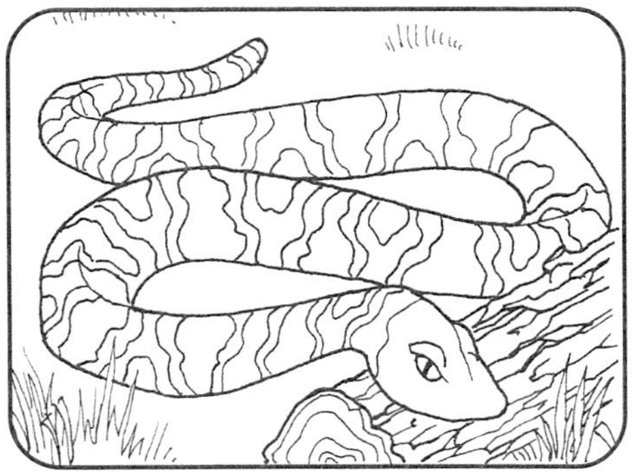

1. When a snake is ready to shed its skin, its eyes turn milky white.

3. The snake slowly wriggles out of its skin.

4. ______________________________
____
____

Name ____________________

Dragon Mountain

Lao Lao lived in a tiny village in China. The village was . . .

Name ______________________

Badger

Design a poster about Badger for the animals to remember him by.

Copymaster 21
Unit 21

Name ______________________

Julian and Huey's Surprise

Who are Julian and Huey planning to surprise? ______________________

____

How are they going to surprise him? ______________________

____

____

What will happen? ______________________

____

____

How will the story end? ______________________

____

____

Name ______________________

Character Profile

Name of character: ______________________

Title of the book he/she is from: ______________________

____

Draw your character here.

Helpful words

old young
kind unkind
lucky unlucky
excited careless
thoughtful lazy
clever foolish
crafty sly
funny happy
miserable

Now write about your character.

____

____

____

____

____

____

____

Copymaster 23
Unit 23

Name ____________________

Question Wheel

Cut out templates A and B.
Place A on top of B.
Now fix A and B together by pushing a paper fastener through the centre.

A

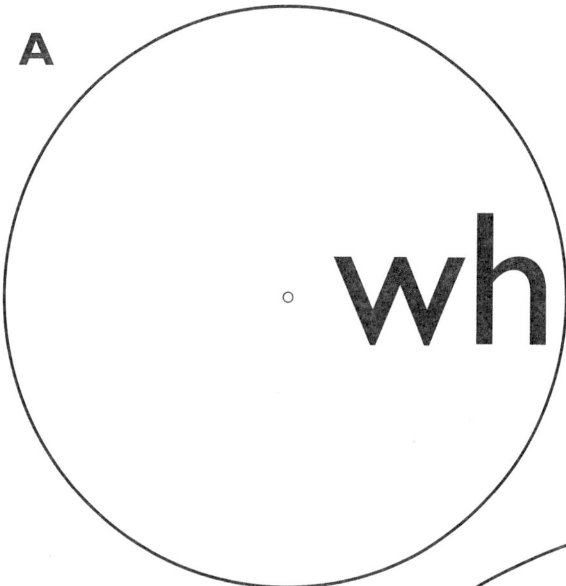

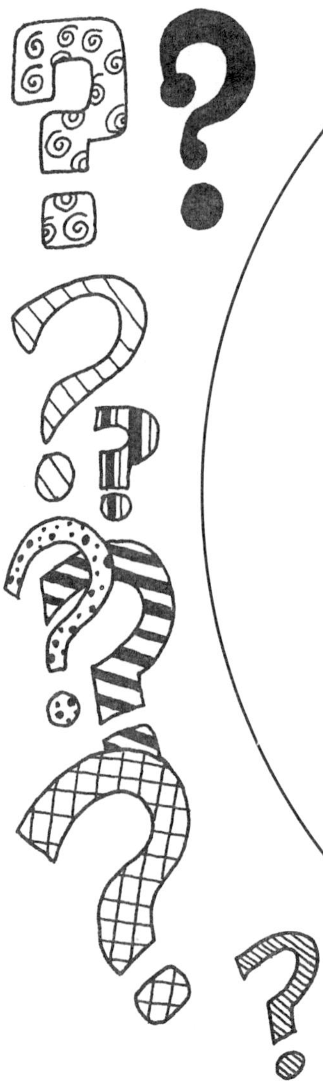

B

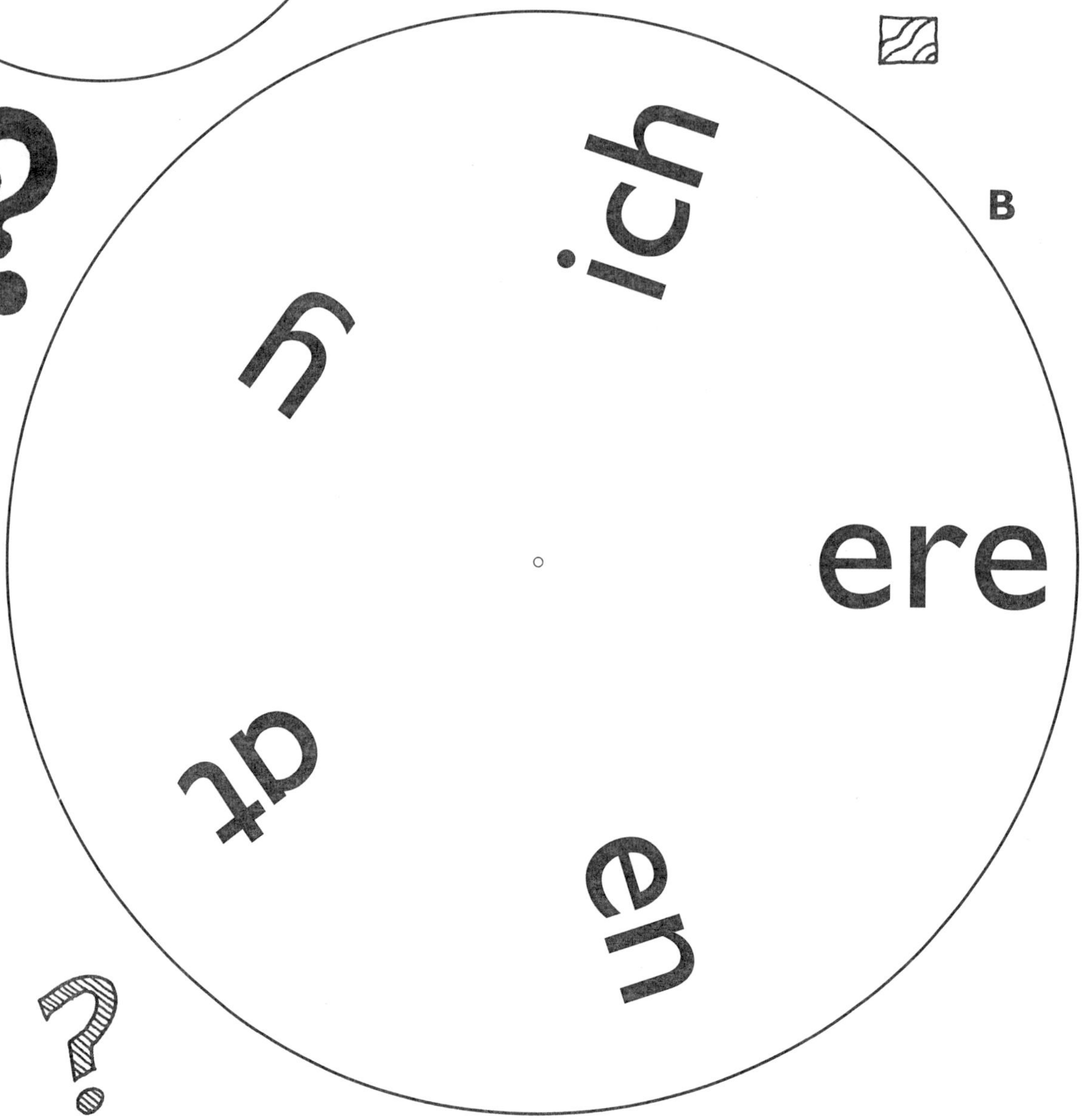

Name

Riddles

Make up some riddles.

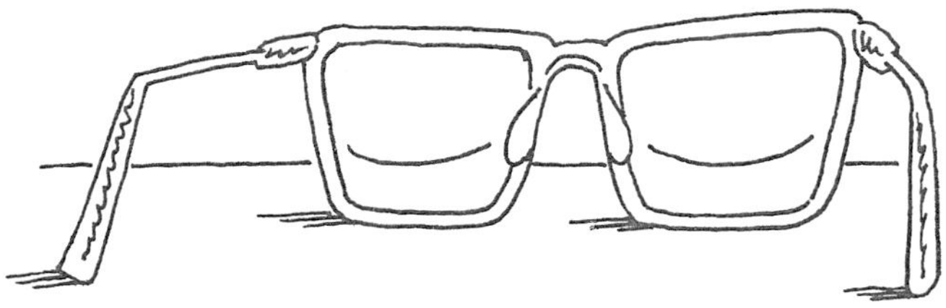

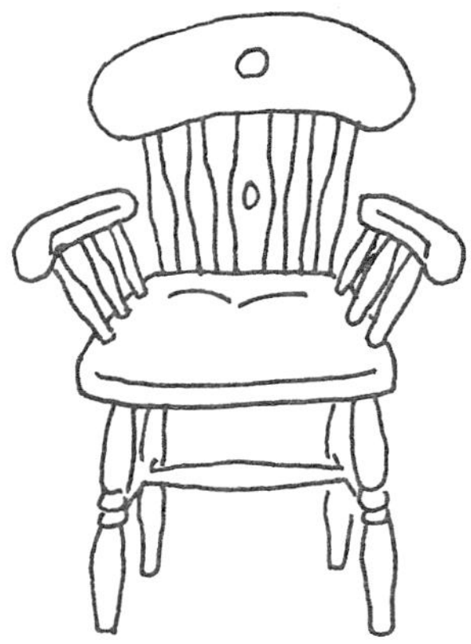

Make up a riddle of your own.

Copymaster 25
Unit 29

Name ____________

Kitchen Machines

Use the words below to label the machines in this kitchen.

cooker **fridge** **microwave** **kettle** **toaster**

Write a definition for each machine.

cooker ____________________

____

fridge ____________________

____

microwave ____________________

____

kettle ____________________

____

toaster ____________________

____

Copymaster 26
Unit 30

Name ______________________

Little Red Riding Hood and the Wolf

In came the little girl in red.
She stopped. She stared and then she said,

____

____

____

____

____

____

Finish the story of Little Red Riding Hood in your own words.

____

____

____

____

____

____

____

____

____

____

Name ______________________

Story Report

Title: ______________________

Author: ______________________

This story was about ______________________

____

____

____

The best bit was when ______________________

____

____

____

My favourite character was ______________________

because ______________________

____

____

____

Colour in the stars to show how much you enjoyed the story.

☆ quite good
☆☆ good
☆☆☆ brilliant

Name ______________________

What Did I Learn This Term?

1. Read the sentences and write **ed** or **ing** in each space.

I play_____ my recorder in assembly last week.

Mum told my baby brother to stop pull_____ my hair.

My friend want_____ to come to my house for tea.

2. Write the words you can make using these letters.

sh		k
d	ar	p
st		t

______________ ______________

______________ ______________

____

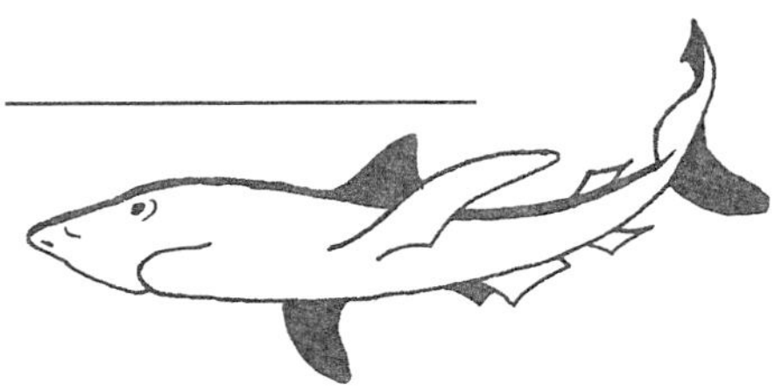

3. The instructions on making a mug of tea are in the wrong order. Number them 1 to 5 so that they are in the correct order.

___ Switch the kettle on.

___ Carefully pour the boiled water onto a tea bag in a mug.

___ Stir the mug of tea adding milk and sugar if you wish.

___ Fill a kettle with water.

___ Take the tea bag out of the mug.

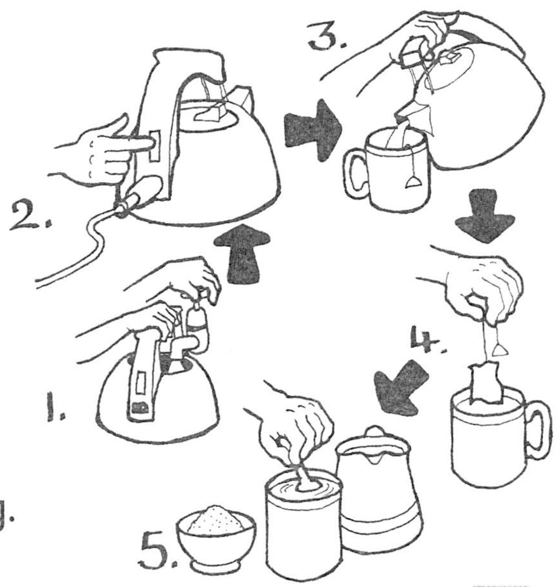

Name ______________________________

Assessment Master TERM 2

What Did I Learn This Term?

1. Read the sentences and write **air**, **or** or **er** in each space.

The robb_____ was sh_____t with spiky h_____.

I think it is unf_____ that my broth_____ is allowed to stay up lat_____ than me.

2. Write a word that means the **opposite** to each of these.

yes	____________	up	____________
hot	____________	big	____________
unhappy	____________	dry	____________

3. Find two smaller words in each of these words.

teapot	____________	____________
dishwasher	____________	____________
football	____________	____________
motorbike	____________	____________

4. Add **commas** where they are needed in this list.

The days of the week are Monday Tuesday Wednesday Thursday Friday Saturday and Sunday.

Assessment Master
TERM 3

Name ______________________

What Did I Learn This Term?

1. Write the correct word in each space.

My sister fell off __________ bike and hurt her arm. **her/his**

I __________ a huge fish in the river last week. **catch/caught**

The children __________ making sand castles. **is/are**

2. Join up the words which mean the same.

big	horrible
wet	large
nasty	shout
yell	damp

3. Add **ful** or **ly** to each of these words.

forget_____	help_____	exact_____
soft_____	care_____	sudden_____

Now write a sentence using one of the words you have made.

____

____

GREAT WORK!

Focus on Literacy 2

ACHIEVEMENT AWARD

Awarded to ______________________________

For ____

Signed ________________ Date ___________

School ______________________________

GREAT WORK!

Focus on Literacy 2

ACHIEVEMENT AWARD

Awarded to ______________________________

For ____

Signed ________________ Date ___________

School ______________________________

RECORD SHEET

NAME ______________________________ CLASS ________

Year 2 • Term 1

Word level work: phonics, spelling, vocabulary

Objective	Comment
Phonological awareness, phonics and spelling **1** Long vowel digraphs	
2 Long vowel phonemes	
3 *oo* (short as in "good"), *ar*, *oy*, *ow*	
4 Words with the same sounds but different spellings	
Word recognition, graphic knowledge and spelling **5** 30 more words from Appendix List 1	
6 High frequency words	
7 Verb endings: *s* (plural), *ed* (past tense), *ing* (present tense)	
8 The terms "vowel" and "consonant"	
9 Spell common irregular words from Appendix List 1	
Vocabulary extension **10** New words	
Handwriting **11** Practise handwriting patterns from Year 1	
12 Use and practise the four basic handwriting joins	

Sentence level work: grammar and punctuation

Objective	Comment
Grammatical awareness **1** Use awareness of grammar to decipher unfamiliar words	
2 Words and phrases that link sentences	
Sentence construction and punctuation **3** Commas and exclamation marks	
4 Re-read own writing for sense	
5 Other uses of capitalisation	
6 Simple organisational devices	

Text level work: comprehension and composition

Objective	Comment
Fiction and poetry ***Reading comprehension*** **1** Applying word-level skills	
2 Predict and check meanings of unfamiliar words	
3 Awareness of difference between spoken and written language	
4 Understand time and sequential relationships in stories	
5 Plot	
6 Discuss familiar themes and link to own experiences	
7 Learn, re-read and recite poems	
8 Collect and categorise poems	
Writing composition **9** Apply phonological, graphic knowledge and sight vocabulary to spelling	
10 Use story structure to write about own experience in similar form	
11 Use language of time to structure a sequence of events	
12 Use simple poetry structures and substitute own ideas	
Non-fiction ***Reading comprehension*** **13** Simple instructions, recipes, plans	
14 Note key structural features	
15 Write simple instructions	
Writing composition **16** Organise instructions sequentially	
17 Use diagrams in instructions	
18 Use appropriate register in writing instruction	

RECORD SHEET

NAME ______________________ CLASS ________

Year 2 • Term 2

Word level work: phonics, spelling, vocabulary

Objective	Comment
Phonological awareness, phonics and spelling **1** Long vowel phonemes	
2 Vowel phonemes: *air, or, er*	
3 Digraphs: *wh, ph, ch* (as in "Christopher")	
4 Split compound words into their component parts	
5 Discriminate, orally, syllables	
Word recognition, graphic knowledge and spelling **6** Read and spell all the words from Appendix List 1	
7 High frequency words	
8 Prefixes: *un-, dis-*	
9 Spell common irregular words	
Vocabulary extension **10** New words	
11 Antonyms	
Handwriting **12** Handwriting patterns from Year 1	
13 Handwriting in conjunction with phonic and spelling patterns above	
14 The four basic handwriting joins	

Sentence level work: grammar and punctuation

Objective	Comment
Grammatical awareness **1** Deciphering new and unfamiliar words	
2 Intonation and expression	
3 Re-read own writing for grammatical sense	
4 Grammatical agreement, matching verbs to nouns/pronouns	
5 Verb tenses	
Sentence construction and punctuation **6** Identify and understand speech marks	
7 Different ways of presenting texts	
8 Use commas in a list	
9 Constructing sentences in different ways, while retaining meaning	
9 Simple sentences	

Text level work: comprehension and composition

Objective	Comment
Fiction and poetry ***Reading comprehension*** **1** Applying word-level skills	
2 Predict and check meanings of unfamiliar words	
3 Discuss and compare story themes	
4 Predict story endings/incidents	
5 Discuss story settings	
6 Identify and describe characters	
7 Re-tell stories individually and through role-play	
8 Read own poems aloud	
9 Discuss features of sound in poems	
10 Comment on and recognise when the reading aloud of a poem makes sense	
11 Discuss favourite poems and poets using correct terminology	
Writing composition **12** Spell words accurately	
13 Use story settings in own writing	
14 Write character profiles	
15 Use structures from poems as a basis for writing	
Non-fiction ***Reading comprehension*** **16** Locate words by initial letter	
17 Definitions and explanations	
18 Other alphabetically ordered texts	
19 Flow charts and cyclical diagrams	
Writing composition **20** Make class dictionaries and glossaries	
21 Produce flow charts or diagrams that explain a process	

RECORD SHEET

NAME ______________________ CLASS ________

Year 2 • Term 3

Word level work: phonics, spelling, vocabulary

Objective	Comment
Phonological awareness, phonics and spelling **1** Phonemic spellings from five previous terms	
2 Discriminating syllables	
3 *ear* (as in "hear") and *ea* (as in "head")	
Word recognition, graphic knowledge and spelling **4** Reading and spelling of high frequency words	
5 Read high frequency words in guided texts	
6 Words with same spelling patterns but different sounds	
7 Common suffixes, e.g. *-ful*, *-ly*	
8 Spell common irregular words	
Vocabulary extension **9** New words	
10 Synonyms	
Handwriting **11** Practise handwriting in conjunction with the phonic and spelling patterns above	
12 Use the four basic handwriting joins in independent writing	

Sentence level work: grammar and punctuation

Objective	Comment
Grammatical awareness **1** Intonation and expression	
2 Grammatical agreement, matching verbs to nouns/pronouns	
3 Use standard forms of verbs	
Sentence construction and punctuation **4** Commas in lists	
5 Accurate use of capital letters and full stops in sentences	
6 Turn statements into questions, learning a range of *wh* words typically used to open questions	
7 Compare various forms of questions	

Text level work: comprehension and composition

Objective	Comment
Fiction and poetry ***Reading comprehension*** **1** Applying word-level skills	
2 Predict and check meanings of unfamiliar words	
3 Notice difference between spoken and written forms	
4 Compare books by same author	
5 Read author information	
6 Respond to humorous stories, extracts, poems	
7 Compare books by different authors on similar themes	
8 Discuss meanings of words and phrases that create humour, and sound effects in poetry, and classify poems	
Writing composition **9** Spell words accurately	
10 Sustained story writing	
11 Use humorous verse as a structure for writing	
12 Book evaluations	
Non-fiction ***Reading comprehension*** **13** Understand distinction between fact and fiction	
14 Pose questions and record in writing prior to reading non-fiction	
15 Use contents page, index	
16 Scan text to find specific sections	
17 Skim-read title, contents page, illustrations, chapter headings and sub-headings	
18 Evaluate usefulness of text for its purpose	
Writing comprehension **19** Make simple notes	
20 Write non-fiction texts	
21 Write non-chronological reports	

Appendix

1

High frequency words to be taught through Year 2

about
after
again
an
another
as
back
ball
be
because
bed
been
boy
brother
but
by
call
came
can't
could
did
dig
do
don't
door
down
first
from
girl
good
got
had
half
has
have
help
her
here
him
his
home
house
how
if
jump
just
last
laugh
little
live
love
made
make
man
many
may
more
much
must
name
new
next
night
not
now
off
old
once
one
or
our
out
over
people
push
pull
put
ran
saw
school
seen
should
sister
so
some
take
than
that
their
them
then
there
these
three
time
too
took
tree
two
us
very
want
water
way
were
what
when
where
who
will
with
would
your

Plus:

- days of the week
- months of the year
- numbers to twenty
- common colour words
- pupil's name and address
- name and address of school